THE WRY WORLD OF REG HENRY

REG HENRY

ISBN: 978-1-63385-013-2
Library of Congress Control Number: 2014917002

Cover and page 192 photos by: Lake Fong/Post-Gazette

Book design by: Jason Price

Published by
Word Association Publishers
205 Fifth Avenue
Tarentum, Pennsylvania 15084

www.wordassociation.com
1.800.827.7903

CONTENTS

PREFACE

From the point of view of the innocent reader, this is all my old Dad's fault. He encouraged me, both to enter journalism and to write a humorous column, hereby compiled into a selection of favorites.

From my point of view, I am glad he did encourage me. Journalism is a fine pursuit, much better than grave digging or other sweaty occupations — and there's a bit of drinking involved.

Writing a weekly humorous column is a great pastime too. It provides a holiday from my regular work, which is composing serious editorials on subjects so boring that police negotiators read them to hostage-takers to make them give up.

Oddly, while most of the columns are an attempt to make you smile, a few of them might make you cry or rage. A personal column has its moods — laughter, tears, anger or spontaneous cuteness. My subject has been life and, as you may have noticed, life has its up and downs.

I started writing the column in 1988. Because the news in newspapers is mostly bad, it began as an exercise in simply trying to cheer up the readers. A little while later I decided I would try to make people think as well as laugh by adding more opinion, particularly on political topics. The result was those who liked me, liked me more, and those who disliked me, disliked me more. Did I say life has its ups and downs?

But the column had two earlier iterations. For about a year, ending in 1985 when I went away on a fellowship, I wrote a column called Oh Henry! Those are lost to posterity and posterity is the better for it. I also contributed to the Saturday Diary and some of those efforts are reproduced here.

I could have arranged this book in chronological order but instead I left chronology to the seven separate chapters. In that way, the newer work is mixed throughout with the old and those who don't like my politics — on the liberal side — can conveniently avoid that chapter (and maybe the one about guns, too), yet still enjoy most of the book. And, yes, I recognize that hope is about as likely as me waggling my ears and becoming airborne.

Actually, though, I have kept politics to a minimum because the topic is so perishable and, besides, I much prefer writing about my family. Over the years, readers have expressed a strong preference for that, too.

In picking what I think are the best of my columns, I consulted with Facebook friends, and asked actual friends in person (thank you, Rich Brandt!). A colleague, Mila Sanina, the most tech-savvy person I know, was able to tell me what columns had registered the most "hits" over the years. But at the end of the day, most of the selections were just intuition.

In addition to those good people, I must thank many others — my bosses and editors at the Pittsburgh Post-Gazette for indulging and helping me, my friend Mike Morsch, a fellow writer in Philadelphia who has served as my pre-publication critic, and the loyal fans of the column and previously my blog who have kept up my spirits.

But the greatest thanks go to my core inspirations, my wife, Priscilla, daughter Allison (also Critter, Tillie and Lucy) and son Jim (and Katie), and of course my Dad (and Mum), whom I wish were still in this world to receive a copy.

Happy reading. It better be happy because there are no refunds.

REG HENRY

August, 2014.

CHAPTER ONE

RANDOM ACTS OF SILLINESS

A FEW WORDS IN DEFENSE OF SEWICKLEY, MY TOWN

Saturday Diary, April 19, 1997

In the great property assessments controversy, no area has received more dubious publicity than the Quaker Valley School District and the borough of Sewickley, which everybody and his dog now knows as the haunt of rich, tax-averse Republicans.

As Sewickley is my town, and as my own house was among those pictured in the Post-Gazette, I thought it only proper that I should be the one to come to its defense against unfair public perceptions.

This is not for my own sake. Having a picture of my home in the paper was only fair, although I wish somebody had told me in advance so that I could have gotten the gardener to cut the hedge.

My motive in defending Sewickley is a matter of setting the record straight. As I remarked to the butler just the other day, the image of the town as a posh person's retreat is a ridiculous stereotype.

Make no mistake: We have lots of Democrats in Sewickley. There's er . . . what-his name . . . and that other fellah.

Oh, it is easy to make fun of our charming little town, but it amounts to nothing more than base jealousy. These dreadful populist types, before they rush off to Mt. Lebanon in the evening, like nothing better than to paint Sewickley folks as so many snobs.

Perhaps it was the introduction of afternoon tea on the 16A Ohio Valley bus, with the fine linen and china, that inflamed the critics. Scoff all you like, but the crumpets are scrumptious and I like the idea that the PAT drivers wear white gloves.

The thing I love about Sewickley is that it is so self-contained.

Geographically, one is reminded of Lord Byron's evocative description of the plain of Marathon: "The mountains look on Marathon and Marathon looks on the sea."

In my little world, Sewickley Heights looks on Sewickley and Sewickley looks on the river.

OK, so it doesn't have the same poetic ring, but it does describe the lay of the land.

I live down in the village. And while it lacks the advantage of fox hunters running through the back yard trampling the petunias, it has just about everything else.

It has a bar, a Chinese restaurant, a library, a hospital, a YMCA and a bagel bakery. Surely the human heart desires nothing more.

In addition, there are wonderful antiques to be seen in Sewickley, not all of them people.

It has its own newspaper, The Herald, where readers happily get themselves into a huge frenzy over small controversies.

Why, Sewickley even has its own web page. I'm not really good at computer stuff, but I believe the address is www. redandgreenpants.com.

The greatest thing about Sewickley is its special character. We do things a little bit differently than other people.

Consider my house, for example (everybody else has). You might think this is the Henry house. You would think wrong.

In Sewickley, it is traditional for your house to be known by the name of its last owner.

For example, when I owned a house in Edgeworth (which is part of the Sewickley postal code), we did not live in the Henry house.

It only became known as the Henry house when we sold it to the Smyth family and moved away. And it only became the Smyth house when they sold it and moved away. In turn, the people who bought the Smyth house must wait until they move before it is named after them - which, of course, is only fair.

Is that perfectly clear? This is all done to avoid confusion, and should certainly help the tax assessors in their work. But this practice does not go on forever, just for a few years - say 30 or 40.

Another oddity is that men, at least married ones, do not have names in Sewickley. For identification purposes, we are mere appendages of our wives.

Some will think this observation outdated or politically incorrect, but in my experience that is how things are.

In Sewickley, I am Priscilla's husband, and there's an end to it. I'm not complaining. That is a very fine thing to be.

It works like this. People will say to me at cocktail parties, "You are Priscilla's husband, aren't you?"

And I will reply: "Yes, and one day I hope to have my own identity."

But to be known as anything else is a forlorn hope any-where near Beaver Street.

I was speaking recently to Beth's husband on this very point. We observed that Maris' husband, Mary Jane's husband, even Candace's husband . . . these are men of grave affairs whose power and renown know no bounds - except when they come home. In Sewickley, they are nothing.

And how do Sewickley women wield their awesome power? In political action, of course. The power-plays, the maneuvering, the behind-the-scenes meetings . . . the paper was right about the strong political flavor of the area.

But this is not Republican politics; this is paddle-tennis politics.

Apparently, a municipal ordinance requires every resident to play some sort of racket sport. Paddle - sometimes called platform - tennis is very popular in the winter months, when passions are running their highest. The politics surrounding this eccentric pastime remind me of the former Yugoslavia, but are less temperate.

But let us not dwell on the darker side on this sunny glen, this suburban Eden, where men are men even if they are known by women's names.

In affirming my local pride, I declare that I have nothing against people in other areas such as Mt. Lebanon, even if it is a serious breach of taste to live there.

My point is that you should not believe all the hurtful stereotypes about this blessed plot, this earth, this realm, this . . . Sewickley. ✿

VISIT A LIVE WORSHIP SHOP TODAY

Column, May 1, 2001

In the little park and plaza outside the Gateway Four Building in Downtown Pittsburgh, a designated smoking area has been set up for the office workers.

Nothing unusual in this concept. Society really wants to drape smokers' necks with signs that say "Smoking Leper Alert: Unclean! Unclean!" But, instead, the hapless smokers are herded into special little areas where passing pedestrians can feel superior to them.

No doubt the smokers feel very ashamed; on the other hand, they get to spend large amounts of time standing outside buildings while the people inside — who have no excuse to leave — have to work. Come to think of it, I may start smoking if the weather gets any nicer.

What makes the Gateway Four smoking area a little different are the portable signs that mark its boundaries. On one side they say: "No Smoking Beyond This Point" and, on the other, "This Is a Smoke-Free Zone."

It is always a cheerful feeling to walk through the plaza and see the smokers puffing away right next to the statement "This Is a Smoke-Free Zone." And why not? This is Pittsburgh, where signs can be wondrous to behold and people can't afford to be too literal.

My favorite sign in the area is the one off Route 65, Ohio River Boulevard, which announces the community of

Bellevue. The sign looks a little like something you might see outside a drive-in theater. On three distinct layers, it says:

Live
Worship
Shop

When I first arrived in Pittsburgh, that sign puzzled me greatly. Back then, signs outside seedy establishments on Liberty Avenue advertised Live Nudes, which was a bit creepy because that suggested the possible existence of dead nudes.

Because there was no Cultural District at the time, just the Live Nude District along Liberty (and presumably the Dead Nude District round the county morgue), I interpreted the Bellevue sign in the same way.

What, I thought, is Live Worship anyway? Is it the opposite of Dead Worship, and is that any way to talk about us Presbyterians?

Whatever Live Worship was, clearly it was popular enough that it needed its own shop to cater to the faithful.

Only later did I realize that it wasn't two adjectives and a noun but three verbal imperatives. Of course! The sign touts Bellevue as a place to live, worship and shop — the big three of human existence.

I am hoping for a similar epiphany that will help me understand those road signs lately erected along our parkways. If you drive, say, into town from the airport, they will nag you in sequence:

Beware of Aggressive Drivers
Slow Down Save a Life

Don't Tailgate

Targeted Enforcement Area

Keep Alert Watch for DUI Drivers

Targeted DUI Enforcement Area

Buckle Up Every Time

Buckle Up It's the Law

Eat Your Vegetables

Practice Safe Sex But Not While Driving

WHEN i FiRST ARRIVED iN PiTTSBURGH

that sign puzzled me greatly. Back then, signs outside seedy establishments on Liberty Avenue advertised Live Nudes, which was a bit creepy because that suggested the possible existence of dead nudes.

OK, I made the last two up, but they are well within the spirit of the thing. Of course, safety would be better served if drivers weren't all reading goofy signs. But hey!

According to the Pennsylvania Department of Transportation in Harrisburg, these signs are part of a pilot program conducted in a number of areas round the state, where authorities have identified repeated problems and wish to draw attention to them. PennDOT says it has agreements with local law enforcement officers to step up patrols in the areas.

My guess is that it's all actually part of a long-running government program called We Got Tons o' Taxpayer Dollars and Feel the Itch to Spend.

What I want to know is, what I am supposed to do when I am fully alert to an Aggressive Driver anyway? Wave a white flag and pull over?

And how come drunks get their own Targeted DUI Enforcement Area while all the rest of us are pulled over in a generic Targeted Enforcement Area?

These are issues to ponder while standing outside city buildings or perhaps visiting Bellevue — indeed, anywhere Pittsburgh area residents gather to reminisce about the Live Nudes of yesteryear. ✤

SNORING IS SUCH UNSWEET SORROW

Column, Dec. 4, 2001

As my subject today is tragedy of a nocturnal sort, it is fitting to open with a quote from Mr. Shakespeare: "To sleep: perchance to dream: ay, there's the rub."

Or as Mrs. Shakespeare might have said: "To sleep, perchance to dream, perhaps to snore. Ay, now there's the rub!" For in any age and in any country, wives tend to think poorly of a husband who snores.

This is most unfortunate, and my aim today is to inspire some sympathy for the plight of the innocent snorer who does not deserve to be berated nightly in his own bed. My plea is particularly pertinent at this time because we are approaching the season of peak snoring activity.

When large holiday meals have worked their magic, the nasal passages tend to become a little narrower as overall the human body takes on a rounder, more jolly appearance.

The phenomenon also seems to be age-related: Nature allows a man to be more dramatic at night when he no longer has the stamina to be so dramatic during the day.

As this festive month advances, bedrooms all over the city and suburbs will turn into veritable bear caves and titanic snores will rattle windows and suck the air round curtains, ruffling the fur on dogs and raising clouds of household dust.

At this signal, women will turn to their husbands and issue those familiar words of endearment: "SHUT UP ALREADY!" Followed by "Thwack," the sound of an object (hand, rolled-up newspaper, baseball bat) hitting the innocent sleeping man.

Consider what my wife said to me just the other night: "For goodness sake, stop breathing!"

If I had my wits about me, instead of being lost in the fog of slumber, I would have said: "Well, darling, I could stop breathing, but you know how you hate funerals."

But I was reduced to falling back on the old standby: "Huh?"

"You are breathing too loudly!" she then explained helpfully.

But of course I wasn't breathing too loudly; she was just listening too closely.

Thwack! Ow!

AS THIS FESTIVE MONTH ADVANCES

bedrooms all over the city and suburbs will turn into veritable bear caves and titanic snores will rattle windows and suck the air round curtains, ruffling the fur on dogs and raising clouds of household dust.

Medical experts warn that snoring can be a symptom of serious health problems and can have dire consequences. But those of us who regularly get beaten up in bed while we sleep already know that.

This is where information about snoring can play a part in reducing marital discord. If only wives knew the facts about snoring, then perhaps they wouldn't feel the need to express their displeasure in such negative ways.

To aid in this, let me explode some of the myths about snoring.

Many wives seem to believe that their slumbering husbands are *deliberately* snoring, that this is an act of free will undertaken to annoy them.

Nothing could be further from the truth. Ladies, when your husbands snore, they are asleep! Yes, asleep — defined as the lack of consciousness.

Hitting them with a 2 x 4 is not helpful in this circumstance. Contrary to what you may believe, they are not lying there in bed with their eyes closed trying to imitate the bark of the Upper Nile hippopotamus, even if they did watch the Discovery channel the previous evening.

As well as a sympathetic understanding of the problem, what is needed is a scientific means to end the nightly symphony. For the moment, the percussion section is the only counter to the wind and brass sections.

Surgery can be performed in some cases, but that is too ghastly to contemplate. A man could lose weight, but that would mean eating less, another horrible prospect in the holiday season.

There is also a spray advertised on TV, but unfortunately that is designed for the snorer to use on himself. A much better idea would be a spray that could render a spouse unconscious, or at least deaf. In that way, a man would be spared the unnatural sensation of coated tonsils.

Perchance I dream: Could not wives consider the snore for what it really is — the mating call of

MANY WIVES

seem to believe that their slumbering husbands are deliberately snoring, that this is an act of free will undertaken to annoy them. Nothing could be further from the truth. Ladies, when your husbands snore, they are asleep! Yes, asleep— defined as the lack of consciousness.

the middle-aged man, the heart lifting a trumpet to sound the eternal call of love? Does it not say: My darling, I breathe yet, and loudly do I proclaim — with great grunts and eccentric lisps — that I abide with you in the dark night, your constant adenoidal admirer and bronchial buckaroo?

Thwack! Ow! On second thought, I guess not. ✦

COLUMNIST'S CRITICS DO HIM A FAVOR: THEY WROTE MOST OF THIS ARTICLE

Dec. 27, 2006

With 2006 almost history, my reading today is taken from The Rubaiyat, wherein the ancient Persian poet gives some timely advice: "Now the New Year reviving old Desires,/ the thoughtful Soul to Solitude retires ..."

Many readers of this column are thoughtful souls and I wish to thank them for their many e-mails, letters and calls this past year. Please know that such thoughtfulness served to boost my ever-threatened morale at timely moments.

My thanks also go to the Scripps Howard News Service, which distributes the column nationally. I know for certain that at least 30 newspapers picked it up this year — but probably the number is double that. It also turns up on various Web sites and blogs.

What does that mean? That I am somehow important? I hope not, because my wife, in the traditional way of wives, has promised that, at the slightest sign of my head swelling, she will hire headhunters from Borneo to come over and shrink it.

That would be a sight: headhunters taking the 16A bus to the borough of Sewickley and walking down Beaver Street with all their head-boiling paraphernalia and inquiring as to my whereabouts among the ladies. You don't see much of that in the suburbs.

No, what all this means is that I get e-mails and letters from Alabama to Alaska. Although the column has many friends, I wish in the New Year for a better class of enemy. Indeed, I appreciate the kind words so much because I also hear regularly from the dyspeptic community.

Now, I am not complaining here. Reaction is oxygen to a writer, even if the oxygen often needs an air freshener. Still, the venom expressed for a column that is usually merry quip and jest, and hopefully many a true word spoken in that jest, is quite remarkable. It seems that many unhappy people live in this country. And while they may have a *sense* of humor, they don't actually possess one.

The other strange thing is that all these e-mails and letters sound the same to me. The complaints have common threads. So in the interests of helping all these unthoughtful souls to solitude, I have put a selection of their comments into one letter so that they may have the last word and some joy come the New Year.

Every word here is from my critics. I have cut and pasted them creatively but the context remains the same — that is to say, I am a big jerk. I do apologize to those left out of the collection. No disrespect is meant; your abuse is much appreciated. Better that you keep me humble than my wife send for the headhunters. Happy New Year to all.

Mr. Henry,

Just read your discombobulated column ... and sat in wonderment of exactly what kind of stuff you're smoking.

As a mother, I found your underwear on your head image juvenile and offensive. Spoken like a true liberal.

Have you ever thought of writing a serious article on health care, perhaps 10,000 or 15,000 words, long enough to earn some respect among serious journalists?

The problem with you is that you are an unpatriotic ingrate. Your hate for President Bush comes shining through in every word you write. Are you ashamed yet? You have the DNC talking points down to a T. You prove it. Liberalism is a mental disease. Get help Henry!

It is so very clear that you are a fundamentalist Christian as you attack what you don't understand. The word "gnostic" does not mean "troublemaker."

EVERY WORD

here is from my critics. I have cut and pasted them creatively but the context remains the same – that is to say, I am a big jerk. I do apologize to those left out of the collection. No disrespect is meant; your abuse is much appreciated.

"Cute liberal atheist" musings! Unfortunately, you and your kind have no answers for the world situation except to "cut and run." I am sure that if the time comes that we are overcome by the terrorists you will be among the first to convert to Islam.

Go back to Australia — we have enough dribbling newspaper columnists here. You are dung from Down Under. Why do you insist on writing trite garbage?

You sound angry. Today's example of your socially divisive writing helps to perpetuate hate, mistrust and misery. You attempt to camouflage your hatred with banal humor and false bravado writing styles.

You must have quite a job! Whining and moaning all the time. So instead of complaining, why don't you, President Henry, come up with your ideas on running the country?

With all due respect, you have not lived in Sewickley long enough to be truly called a "Sewickleyite."

Regards ... ✤

LORDY, LORDY, LOOK WHO'S 40!

Column, May 16, 2007

Like a benediction said at the Tomb of the Unknown Wrinkle, today's column is dedicated to the aging process, so named because it takes our mortal meat and processes it until we resemble an old salami. With this cheerful thought in mind, these words are also meant as a birthday bouquet to Angie (Bellisario) Ocilka of Elizabeth Township.

As I do not get out much, I have never met Angie or spoken to her, but I have it on good report that she is a great person and today she turns 40.

The good report comes from her sister-in-law, Lynn Ocilka of Bethel Park, who out of the blue sent me an e-mail. "Dear Mr. Henry," it said, "I don't know if you recall speaking to Shamrock Manor Women's Club in Bethel Park a couple of years ago? ..."

The old mind goes misty. Wait, was that the time that the secular version of Pentecostal fire lit up the hall and moved the ladies to rapturous delight, setting sensible shoes tapping to the steady beat of my every witticism?

No, come to think of it, that happens only in my dreams. In truth, I have only a vague recollection of Shamrock Manor Women's Club, just a sense of nice people who had the good manners not to throw anything at the speaker. The absence of projectiles is always my definition of a successful speech.

It was apparently so successful that it prompted Lynn Ocilka to make a request unprecedented in my years of writing columns. She wanted to go beyond the traditional "Lordy, lordy, looks who's 40" classified ad arranged by relatives and friends who believe that bad poetry is good for an aging person's complexion. She wanted me to write something about her sister-in-law in the paper.

As she put it, "My sister-in-law is turning 40 on May 16th. This is the same sweet soul who on my 40th birthday announced 'You will turn 50 before I turn 40, Ha, ha, ha.' "

Of course, it was a crazy request. What am I, some sort of journalistic short-order cook? On the other hand, when it comes to ha, ha, ha, I fancy myself as the man for the job.

Besides, I remember fondly the late Joe Browne, who wrote a column called "Our Towne" for the Post-Gazette for more than 20 years and was beloved by all — except the postman who had to deliver his mountain of mail. Joe only worked late at night for a few hours and would glean tidbits from readers' letters and make an amusing column. (This was before the Lord sent the Bush administration as a gift to columnists and other cynics.)

Joe, who died in 1994, had a great sense of humor and I reckon he had this journalism business figured out, although I may be biased because he always had a kind word for me when I was just a young rim rat on the copy desk. Joe knew something many newspapers have forgotten: It is the so-called ordinary people who are extraordinary.

So here's to you, Angie Ocilka, whom my old mate Joe would have celebrated for entering the realm of the ancient if he were still here. Here's to you, extraordinary married mother of three boys.

Angie, I am sorry that I could not have warned you about this but your sister-in-law said you would approve. Anyway, who wouldn't be pleased about having their decrepitude announced to the whole world? A person would have to be very touchy to object.

So let me put your fears about the aging process to rest. True, your body may soon resemble a government department — slow, inefficient and uncoordinated. But you are not to blame for this physical decline. Actually, Sir Isaac Newton is to blame. As you know, he invented gravity, a word suspiciously close to grave, which gravity does its eternal best to level us into.

It is a well-known scientific fact that gnarly gnomes live under our beds and emerge to do the work of gravity while we sleep. They love to swing on our body parts and stretch them mercilessly. Women with their shapely bits are at particular risk and the only antidote is to crack jokes in your sleep until the gnomes go away. (Gnomes are known to be particularly grumpy because during the day they listen to talk radio.)

Today, Angie, all of us in the wrinkled community will join me in wishing you a happy 40th birthday!

Alas, the rest of you people will have to grow old without my mentioning it. Joe Browne is with the saints and my business is still with the sinners. ✤

IT IS A WELL-KNOWN SCIENTIFIC FACT

that gnarly gnomes live under our beds and emerge to do the work of gravity while we sleep. They love to swing on our body parts and stretch them mercilessly. Women with their shapely bits are at particular risk ....

THANK-YOU NOTES: THE LAST HOPE OF CIVILIZATION

Column, July 25, 2007

Today's column is about class and American society. Please do not run for the hills immediately because I write as a man of the people. Maybe you will thank me later.

The question of the day is: What makes a classy person in the best sense of the word? Wearing an ascot and looking a perfect chump at a cocktail party won't do it, even if you complete your ensemble with red or green pants decorated with little whales.

Yet, I myself have been tempted on occasion to don an ascot for a night out and was only saved by a spousal death-ray stare.

You see, as a resident of Sewickley, where being classy is required by municipal ordinance (I believe it's in the same statute as compulsory paddle tennis playing and the ownership of yellow Labs), I do feel the need to go to absurd lengths to show that I have arrived.

Admittedly, this is silly. It's not very hard to arrive — you can take the 16A bus to get there, but that apparently won't do.

Still, as an outsider observing classy people and the great pretenders who seek to walk in their loafers, I have come to understand a thing or two about proper social behavior.

This is what I know: Class is not about riches, fine tailoring, good schooling, correct use of forks at dinner parties and the rest of it, although some posh persons would have you believe otherwise.

No, at the end of the day, when the cocktail hour comes around and the mind becomes mellow enough to make proper judgments, what separates the nouveau riche, the parvenu, the social climber or crawler, the bounder and the Pittsburgh Tribune-Review reader from the truly classy person is the writing of personal thank-you notes.

True class is about thoughtfulness, not income. It is about saying "please" and "thank you," and writing down "thank you" later just in case your hosts were deaf.

Mothers, according to the song, should not let their babies grow up to be cowboys. What I am saying is that it doesn't matter that they grow up to be cowboys as long as they have been taught to write thank-you notes. ("Dear Bull: Thank you for a wonderful ride. I do hope my spurs did not give offense.")

Everywhere in modern life the gentle customs and civilized practices are under siege, even in Sewickley, and the writers of thank-you notes stand athwart this depressing tide. The barbarians may be at the gates, but the home guard of civilization must first write thank-you notes for past kindnesses before they deal with the unpleasantness.

This is very good and its virtue only came clear to me the other day. From time to time, I speak to community groups desperate for entertainment. In the question-and-answer period at a residence for senior citizens out in Oakmont, a lady asked me whether I thought the sending of e-mails would spell doom for the U.S. Postal Service.

No, I said, as long as the good people of Sewickley are sending their thank-you notes, and by extension decent folks in other places in America are applying themselves to embossed stationery where civilization still holds sway, then the Postal Service is safe from ruin.

To be sure, it is tough on the carriers. I see them manfully trudging down Beaver Street, their bags bulging with thank-you notes, as the yellow Labs and golden retrievers bark a doleful chorus. They are consoled in knowing that they are the last messengers of good manners.

Truly, the proud boast can be said of these noble workers: Neither snow nor rain nor heat nor the residue of a heavy social calendar can stay these couriers from the swift completion of their appointed rounds.

You think I mock. No, I do not mock. I sincerely admire the habit of thank-you note writing. It takes great talent to write the perfect thank-you note. Haiku and sonnet writing are as nothing compared to this. For all my art and craft, I cannot write a good thank-you note to save myself. I can never think of what to say after, you know, "thank you." That is why I remain an ingrate without any class.

Despite what I told that nice lady in Oakmont, I fear that it may yet happen that mothers do not pass on the thank-you note tradition to their children. Worse yet, the children might learn the protocol imperfectly and start e-mailing or — horror of horrors — begin text messaging their thank-you notes.

Then, the rough beast, its hour come round at last, will slouch toward the post office to be undelivered. No thank you. ✱

> **TO BE SURE,** *it is tough on the carriers. I see them manfully trudging down Beaver Street, their bags bulging with thank-you notes, as the yellow Labs and golden retrievers bark a doleful chorus. They are consoled in knowing that they are the last messengers of good manners.*

VIVE LA FRANCE, AND THE FRENCH

Column, Oct. 10, 2007

When George W. Bush was putting together his Coalition of the Willing — or, in some cases, the Coalition of the Not Very Willing but We Better Do It Not to Offend America — France was a notable nonstarter for the invasion of Iraq.

Although France sent troops to Afghanistan, this shrugging "*non*" was greeted on this side of the Atlantic with all the sympathy and understanding of a great nation — that is to say, with one thunderous Bronx cheer from sea to shining sea.

Everywhere under spacious skies the amber waves of grain swayed with the force of the collective American hissy fit. Those *fromage*-loving ingrates! This is what we get for saving their stylish butts in World War II? How dare they show national independence? We'll show them!

And, mesdames and messieurs, we did show them. Our wrath burned to such childish extremes that french fries were renamed freedom fries in patriotically confused circles.

Some American grown-ups raised timid objections amid all the talk of surrender monkeys and disparaging references to French plumbing. Yes, the bidet does have its surprises and it's been a while since a French victory in life's military playoffs. But, hey, Napoleon wasn't Monsieur Cut and Run, nor were the heroes of Verdun.

I remember saying as much to my vacationing in-laws up in the Adirondacks at the height of the anti-French feeling over Iraq. On a warm summer evening, my tongue loosened somewhat by alcoholic beverages, as sometimes happens, I made the mistake of observing that, despite their less-than-glorious motives in opposing the war with Saddam, the French were basically right — entering the Iraqi snake pit was folly.

Well, all the family turned on me as one and denounced me as the sort of perfidious fellow who would eat Camembert in bed. They said my supposed pals the French had the backbones of flaky croissants.

Now, I am not one to tell people I dearly love that I told you so in light of all that has happened since. Just for the record, however, I would like to deny the allegation that I eat Camembert in bed. (Brie, maybe.)

The amazing thing is that it seems France is back in America's good books. Sure, some Americans still fondle their anti-Gallic grievances like security blankets but at least we no longer suffer political indigestion over french fries. We have grown up *un peu*.

I think this change of heart has something to do with France electing a new president, Nicolas Sarkozy, who is unbashedly pro-American despite all our French-bashing. He even spent a vacation this summer at Lake Winnipesaukee in New Hampshire. President Bush *et famille* had him over for lunch in Maine, which was right neighborly.

But, for me, the real sign that *le bon temps* of Franco-American relations are rolling again is that my beloved family of erstwhile rabid French-bashers took a vacation over there last week, *moi* included. The visit was prompted by the oldest of four sisters and one brother turning 60. The rendezvous was Provence in the south of France.

The virtues of Provence are well-known, thanks and no thanks to Peter Mayle's books, starting with "A Year in Provence." Of course, he should have shut up. Writing literary

THE AMAZING

thing is that it seems France is back in America's good books. Sure, some Americans still fondle their anti-Gallic grievances like security blankets but at least we no longer suffer political indigestion over french fries. We have grown up un peu.

love notes to lovely locales inevitably attracts tourists. Wearing shorts and popping gum in cathedrals, they descend like termites in ball caps to eat up the local charm.

Still, with *le chat* well and truly out of the bag, I can say that Provence is beautiful. The ancient villa we rented was set between a field of olive trees and vineyards heavy with fruit. Soaring Mount Ventoux, with its bald summit, which made me instantly fond of it, looked down upon the scene, which included the charming little village of St. Didier, where we ate our breakfasts of *cafe au lait* and baguettes.

The people were the greatest revelation. They seem not to have noticed we were mad at them. They were kind, pleasant and helpful — *toujours*. True, a couple of times, an international signal involving the finger was given in incidents concerning cars, but the traffic on a personal level of interaction was *tres agreable*.

This warm reception got me wondering whether our past grievances aren't more like a family dispute. Like it or not, France and the United States are bound at the hip by history — they are our cousins and not always kissing cousins. Without France's help in the American Revolution, October's baseball heroes would be playing cricket. *Mon dieu!*

If we were a mature people — huh! — we might realize we made monkeys of ourselves in the great french fry fiasco when we should have been looking at the big picture and surrendering to our inner cheese of wisdom. ✳

THE SULLY LOOK IS HOT. (RIGHT?)

Column, Feb. 18, 2009

Until my son Jim pointed it out, I did not realize that I have the timely good fortune to have the trendy Sully look. "You got the mustache, Dad, and the silver hair thing going on," he said.

Sully is Chesley B. Sullenberger, the gallant US Airways captain who did not ruffle a single gray hair in calmly ditching Flight 1549 in New York's Hudson River last month after his aircraft struck birds and lost power.

In truth, my look is not what might be called the full Sully. The real deal is a trimmer version of myself — or, more to the point, I am a more wide-bodied version of himself.

We are roughly the same age — he's 58 and I'm 61. Although Sully's hair has not ebbed to the same extent as mine, we both have good growth on the sides of our heads. Unfortunately, this lends me a more koala-like appearance, which might work better if I were a pilot for Qantas.

The Sully look is essentially a dapper, competent look for the mature male. With one great splashdown, Sully has rescued "dapper" from the sartorial clutches of ascot-wearing twits with real or pretend English accents.

Indeed, I believe it will soon be acceptable for meatpackers, iron workers and lumberjacks to be considered dapper without their pals searching their lunch boxes for signs of foie gras and little cucumber sandwiches.

Of course, the Sully look requires first and foremost a decent mustache. When it comes to under-nose deportment, I have the advantage on those callow youths with Sully-like ambitions.

To be sure, I did not hold my own mustache in the highest regard for many years. I treated it as if it were merely an eyebrow that came down for a drink. While I tried to let it grow down at the tips to effect a Mexican bandito appearance, this made me look more like a wayward cactus than anything else.

The Sully mustache — let us call it the Sullytache — is trim and efficient. Its bristles do not curl under stress. This is just the look a man needs on the glide path to the inevitable ditching in the River Styx at the end of life's flight.

It doesn't matter that Sully's life and mine bear little resemblance to each other's beyond our mutually gallant and dapper appearance. Sully was a fighter pilot; in my own military service, I was in charge of strategic drinking and the writing of press releases.

In his job as a pilot, Sully must make life-or-death decisions at the controls. As a journalist, I sometimes

THE SULLY LOOK

is essentially a dapper, competent look for the mature male. With one great splashdown, Sully has rescued "dapper" from the sartorial clutches of ascot-wearing twits with real or pretend English accents.

will try to land a sentence with a dangling participle, hardly a life-or-death event, although you would think it was the way some readers go on about it.

Another difference between Sully and myself is that he is now justly celebrated as a hero everywhere he goes, whereas the celebrations for me are justly muted as always. That's OK. I didn't play in the Super Bowl either, but I wore a No. 43 Steelers jersey to a party.

In today's world, it's the look that counts and Sully has given a certain great image to men of a certain age. Yes, I am certain of it.

The Sully look says: This gray hair and seasoned stature speak not of ruin and decay but of experience and unflappability. As this is Fashion Week in New York City, I would hope that the Sully look comes down from the catwalk-cum-tarmac and spreads into Middle America.

You see, we more-than-middle-aged men have waited a long time for a good look we could embrace and call our own. We were cute once — in my case, for about 5 minutes in 1953 — but then we were led astray by different role models.

We covered our heads so completely with hair cream that flies would get stuck there in the summer, we grew sideburns so long that weed-wackers had to be employed to trim them. Then came The Beatles to confuse everything. If the nights were not so dark, some of us would never have gotten dates.

And now, not a decade too soon and as a shock to our wrinkles, comes the Sully look to make-over our appearance. So let the various birds of life strike — receding gums, widening waistlines, prostate peculiarities — we are looking and feeling good, with mustaches in the downward and locked position.

Ladies, I would just like to say to you: Leave your controls in my capable hands. I would like to say this but I just got a call from my tower ordering me to retract my undercarriage and return to my home field, otherwise she will pour a river of cold water on my venerable head. Suffering Sullytache. ✳

FREEDOM'S JUST ANOTHER WORD FOR WOODSTOCK

Column, July 29, 2009

The only person I know who went to Woodstock 40 years ago is also one of the most conservative people I know. Yes, Tom, that would be you, if you are reading.

Unfortunately, Tom is probably not reading this, because the last time I checked he reads only those publications that Genghis Khan might have favored over breakfast.

By the way, Tom is also one of the nicest people I know, a real prince of a man. It goes to prove that a person's politics aren't always a reliable guide to their essential goodness.

You just don't want to invite Tom over for a dinner party. We did that once and our other guests fled into the night, muttering oaths. I believe they took offense to his comment about DDT being good for the environment, a subject I'm guessing he didn't bring up at Woodstock.

The 40th anniversary of Woodstock is only a couple of weeks away — the several days of peace, love and music began on Aug. 15, 1969, at Max Yasgur's dairy farm. (One oddity of the Woodstock festival was that it was not held in Woodstock but in Bethel, N.Y., but, hey, they were hippies, not geographers.)

In the next few weeks, the news media are likely to feature Woodstock anew, but you should not conclude from this that journalism is entirely populated by old hippies. Well, not entirely. If it were so infested, everybody would forget to do something about the anniversary and say "what a bummer" when they found out afterwards.

No, we in the news media just love anniversaries. It's how we get high. There's nothing like an anniversary. The facts are long established and you just have to harvest them.

The Post-Gazette got in early and did a splendid job in its Sunday Magazine. A particularly interesting feature was a look at the many performers at Woodstock.

It was a shock to see that many of them are now in their 60s. (I don't know why it was a shock to me; I have mirrors in my house.) Of course, some of them are dead, which is an even worse bummer than being a geezer rocker.

For people of a certain age, i.e., certain of their physical ruin, the Woodstock anniversary is a time of introspection as much as nostalgia. Here was the great festival of a generation and 40 years later its meaning touches those who did go and those who didn't.

My excuse for not going was that I was in Australia. The drums I listened to were not beating about love but war. I had not dropped out but had dropped in — right into the army. In six months, I would be in Vietnam, another generational festival of sorts.

So I missed out and part of me regrets this. I liked the music. I liked the freedom and excitement. On the other hand, I would not have liked the huge crowd, the rain, the mud and the garbage. Worse yet, from all reports, pot was plentiful at Woodstock but port-a-potties weren't.

Where have all the flower children gone, long time passing? Around the country, you will still find some old bald hippies with paunches and ponytails accompanied by their old hippie ladies with long hair and no bras (for both sexes, not a good look 40 years on, because while you can resist the system you can't beat gravity).

But mostly I think that many at Woodstock were like young Tom, who went into the stockbroking business.

In August 1969, many Americans were in open rebellion. The war was dragging on, racial unrest was high, and people looked into the abyss of sex and drugs and then largely turned back. My guess is that the port-a-potties, which no amount of flower petals could deodorize, brought them back from the brink to a more traditional, ordered life with good plumbing.

The pendulum swung back. Just a little over a decade later, Ronald Reagan was elected president. Soon you could walk along a road and — unlike the famous song about Woodstock — find not a child of God but a child of accountancy.

As Janis Joplin used to sing, "freedom's just another word for nothing left to lose." But for most Americans the reverse seems more true — freedom's just another word for everything left to gain.

Woodstock was nothing if not an experiment in freedom, but those who came later and supported Ronald Reagan were also motivated by freedom as they sincerely understood it. That argument about freedom — What does it mean? What are the limits? — is every generation's struggle. That music of America's soul has never died. Yeah, I know — like, heavy, man.

THE PENDULUM SWUNG BACK.

Just a little over a decade later, Ronald Reagan was elected president. Soon you could walk along a road and — unlike the famous song about Woodstock — find not a child of God but a child of accountancy.

SOMETHING WORTH MORE THAN PRESENTS

Column, Dec. 23, 2009

Perhaps it was the Three Wise Men who started all the trouble. They brought presents with them when they followed the star to Bethlehem to see the baby Jesus.

Ever since, we have been giving presents to each other to celebrate the holiday, although in truth people in many cultures find excuses to give gifts, much to the joy of store owners.

In the Christmas story, the Three Wise Men brought gold, frankincense and myrrh. Gold is still very acceptable, frankincense and myrrh less so. (For one thing, these items are hard to find at Wal-Mart.)

If the three kings of Orient had been as wise as advertised, they might have brought a stout broom to the stable, but in any age it's hard to know what people need.

One of the sadnesses of growing older is that there comes a time when you don't feel the need for any more presents. You become gifted out.

When you are young, Santa can gift-wrap a brick and make you happy. "Oh, oh, a brick!" you shout, clapping your tiny hands with glee.

> IF THE THREE KINGS OF ORIENT had been as wise as advertised, they might have brought a stout broom to the stable, but in any age it's hard to know what people need.

As you grow older, the happy scene is repeated in different ways, "Oh, oh, a toy car!" or "Oh, oh, an electric train!" (my favorite at age 13).

Yet, sadly, the freshness of early Christmas Day excitement slowly wanes as the years go by. Sure, it is always nice to receive a sweater, a tie or socks — these are useful gifts and reassuring tokens that somebody cares — but year after year, something that might be called sweater fatigue sets in. It is probably a sign of being spoiled but, after a while, it's hard to clap hands and say, "Oh, oh, a sweater!"

My father, who lived in Australia, was 96 when he died and in his final years it was nearly impossible to buy him a suitable Christmas gift. His eyes were not what they were, so a book was hard to read. He didn't need power tools or a tennis racket — and, as you can imagine, roller skates were out.

At my wit's end. I bought him underwear because he needed a supply. Yes, there's nothing like a pair of festive underpants, but even then he did not clap his old hands in joy. He did not shout: "Oh, oh, underpants!"

He had moved beyond presents. What he needed was *presence,* mine and others, family and friends, and, yes, according to his faith tradition, the One whose birthday was being celebrated.

Perhaps the Wise Men knew this. It wasn't the gold, frankincense and myrrh that were important. It was simply their presence for the adoration.

To be honest, I am not ancient enough myself to reject material gifts. If someone wants to be give me a bottle of Veuve Clicquot champagne, scenes of seasonal merriment are guaranteed. Why, after a bottle of that fine vintage it is possible that any underpants given as gifts will be worn on my head in the traditional way of Aussies having a good time.

But however wreathed in bubbles, my mind always goes back 40 years to when my best Christmas gifts — the toy car, the electric train — were still fresh in memory. I was 22. The Vietnam War was going on and, being young and stupid, I had renounced my deferment to take part in it.

Although my regular duties as a soldier were not heroic, I once stayed a couple of days at a fire support base, where small kids would come to the wire to beg rations in between the booming of the artillery. That was pitiable enough.

But it wasn't that which jolted me to the core: On frail strings, as if childhood innocence hung by a thread, those poor Vietnamese kids were pulling little cars made from sardine tins with bottle caps as wheels.

For the first and only time in that tragic land, I, who had enjoyed all the advantages of a comfortable childhood with its many bountiful birthdays and Christmases, cried under the weight of my blessings.

Materialism is our blessing and our curse, as the commercial side of Christmas bears testimony. Too often, the promise of peace on Earth and goodwill among men seems to have been postponed until further notice. But we can do something about that by following the highest star of the human heart.

All I want for Christmas is to be home with my family. All I want is for the servicemen and women to come home safely, their duty done. All I want is for the lonely to be visited, neglected parents to be called and estranged friends to be reunited. Presents are fine, presence is better. Merry Christmas. ✸

BAD CASE OF SEASONAL PHEW DEVELOPING

Column, Jan. 13, 2010

A quotation attributed to Mark Twain insists that "Everybody talks about the weather but nobody does anything about it." Actually, it is doubtful he ever wrote or said this, but the person who did wasn't as funny or as famous. So there.

As it happens, someone has done something about it. That someone is me. It wasn't much of a thing but it was something.

To rebuff the elements and to console the frozen, I kept a diary during the recent harsh winter spell that gripped the nation and sent icy blasts up people's trouser legs, forming icicles on their undershorts, much to the consternation of wannabe underpants bombers.

Day One: What a pleasant and picturesque scene the winter provides! The snow falls gently as if driven by zephyrs, coating the trees with an exquisite gloss. Every home takes on the appearance of a Currier & Ives calendar. All are snug under the blanket of snow.

Why, I bet Mom is inside making cookies and Dad, ever the traditionalist, is away at the store, buying ample supplies of bread and toilet paper, because the good folks at Storm Warning Alert Tracker Calamity have predicted in their newscasts a bit of a cold front.

Day Two: How lucky we are to have seasons! Pity the poor people in Australia, where it is hot and folks have to drag

41

themselves to the beach due to social pressure. Pity the poor Aussie girls who can't afford a different bikini every day so hardly wear anything when they go surfing. They are missing all the winter fun!

Why, I think I shall have a cup of cocoa and blow my nose.

Day Three: No point in sitting around inside counting my blessings. It is time to shovel the sidewalk. Some people have snow blowers but those are for snow wimps. Purists like myself do it with a snow shovel, the most honest of seasonal implements.

This is the way the pioneers did it. They got out their snow shovels and got the wagon train moving again. Nothing stops the joy of shoveling — except, of course, the occasional heart attack or back spasm. But, I say, no pain, no gain.

Day Four: My, the sidewalk is long. It seemed quite short in the summer. However, I am proud of my handiwork. My sweeps with the snow shovel make me a veritable Norman Rockwell of the frozen arts. No salt for me — that would not only destroy the environment but also the aesthetics of the winter moment.

A cheerful neighbor — a ruddy-faced Republican — yells out, "Hey, Reg, tell Al Gore to send over some global warming, will ya!" Ha, ha, ha!

I join in the merry joke. I could point out that unusual weather is predicted in climate change theory and that weather is not climate. But such fellows have so few good jokes that it seems churlish to raise an objection. Besides, a public relations problem does lurk here — if there is not enough snow, it is global warming, and if there is too much snow, it is global warming. I shovel on, but the joy has gone out of it.

Day Five: That's odd. It is snowing again. Will it ever stop? I swear someone came and made the sidewalk longer during the night. It is getting increasingly hard to shovel it before I go to work. The wind has picked up.

I decide that it might be better to take the bus. Good thing I don't. When the old 16A passes by, I see that it has been replaced by a dog sled with the passengers sitting on the back. The wind moans. I have a slight pain in my chest. Is that a heart attack or did the cocoa go down the wrong way?

Day Six: Woke up this morning to find a wolf in the kitchen. It must be a friend of my dog Sooner. What big eyes it has! What big teeth! As he is so big and strong, maybe he could help me shovel the sidewalk, which is now the length of the average airport runway.

When I go out to pour the recently purchased two tons of salt on the sidewalk, I see a polar bear lumber by. It is followed shortly afterward by a pursuing Eskimo with spear in hand.

"What place is this?" the Eskimo inquires.

WOKE UP THIS MORNING to find a wolf in the kitchen. It must be a friend of my dog Sooner. What big eyes it has! What big teeth! As he is so big and strong, maybe he could help me shovel the sidewalk, which is now the length of the average airport runway.

"Sewickley, Pennsylvania," I holler back.

"Ah, we have 100 words for snow in my language but only one word for Sewickley," he says enigmatically.

"And is that word 'spoiled'?" I ask. But he cannot hear me through his earmuffs as he disappears into the blizzard.

Day Seven: Bread and toilet paper supply has run out. Wind howling. Despair mounting. Rip up Currier & Ives calendar to make fire. ✤

LET'S ALL DRINK TO GUINNESS ... OR NOT

Column, May 25, 2011

While a cheering sight, the pictures of President Barack Obama having a pint of Guinness in an Irish pub on Monday left me feeling sorry for myself as a member of a hitherto unidentified group of societal victims.

I consider Guinness to be the very nectar of the Irish gods. What sane adult wouldn't want a Guinness? If not the liquid soul of Ireland, the black beverage crowned with creamy foam is at least a goodly lubricant of all the poetry, humor and spirituality of the Irish people.

I have heard that Guinness makes a fine lunch, too — probably better than my usual salad, which lacks a frothy head, as much as I shake the balsamic dressing bottle.

To see Mr. O'bama knock back his Guinness in four slurps, well, it was one of those moments that made me proud to be an American. One of you conservative fellahs is going to say that he needed a Teleprompter to do the slurping but nothing spoils the moment for me.

Why, I feel like going down to the nearest Irish pub to recreate the scene. There's just one little problem. I don't like the taste of Guinness. I just like the idea of Guinness.

That is the special sorrow for people like me. I expect that millions of us are out here suffering silently. We have been pressured by society into liking certain cultural icons that we don't actually like.

TO SEE
MR. O'BAMA

knock back his Guinness in four slurps, well, it was one of those moments that made me proud to be an American. One of you conservative fellahs is going to say that he needed a Teleprompter to do the slurping but nothing spoils the moment for me.

As this syndrome has never been described before, it falls to me to name it — Wish We Did Syndrome. I know the WWDS sounds like the call sign of a country music station, but our hearts have been cruelly broken, too.

Every WWDS sufferer will have his or her list of things that they would really like to like but don't. Being a vintage journalist, I am also ashamed of not liking Scotch whisky.

A fine single malt whisky is said to be a glorious thing that opens up the heavens so that choirs of kilted angels sing for the drinker. Not for me, they don't. Scotch tastes like cough mixture to me, although apparently it is good for coughs — also porridge poisoning, damp knees and sporran chafing.

Still, I would like nothing better than to sit back in a dimly lit club with a glass of scotch or Guinness in hand, listening to really good jazz. This is America's authentic art form, a vibrant strand plucked from the nation's rich cultural tapestry.

You guessed it. I don't like jazz either. I know jazz is wonderful, but to me it sounds like forgetful musicians trying to find their way back to the tune after several glasses of scotch.

At least it doesn't move me to dancing, which, being rhythm-challenged, I don't like doing. Sure, I would like to be a good dancer, with women marveling at my moves, but

I couldn't dance if my pants were on fire. Women are left to marvel at my inertia.

With the rug safe from me cutting it up, I would like to be a bird watcher, traversing forest and field with binoculars on the trail of the tufted titmouse or the common loon, the only bird known to nest in radio talk show studios.

The sheer eccentricity of the pastime appeals to me, yet once again the reality is not so appealing. You watch the bird. The bird watches you. That's it. Time to go home for an acceptable drink.

One note of hope for WWDS sufferers: Tastes do change. For years, I wanted to like lasagna but didn't. There is social pressure to like lasagna because it is a food often volunteered for potluck dinners. I am sure someone will helpfully bring a lasagna to a Memorial Day picnic near you. Lasagna is cheap, familiar and feeds lots of people.

But it seemed to me a primitive food on the evolutionary tree of pasta, not yet one thing or the other, neither strands of spaghetti nor pieces of penne. I just didn't like its sprawling, saucy attitude.

I got over my distaste eventually, although even today I don't clap my hands in glee and shout "lasagna, lasagna" when the casserole dish arrives.

It's time for WWDS sufferers to come out of the shadows and form a support group. Why, there is probably some poor unfortunate in Pittsburgh who wants to like football or hockey, but doesn't, and is crying out for sympathy and understanding. Unfortunately, nothing can be done in such extreme cases of deviancy, but for everybody else help is at hand.

Of course, it may require a field trip to Ireland, where the Guinness is said to taste better. I know a fellow named O'Henry who would like to lead it. ✿

MY LIFE OF JUBILEE WITH QUEEN ELIZABETH

Column, June 06, 2012

Queen Elizabeth II has been celebrating her Diamond Jubilee in London, and it would be churlish of me not to say "Hip, hip, hooray" to mark the occasion.

As it happens, she and I go way back. In fact, and not to boast, we have crossed paths several times, although she always seems not to recognize me. That's good breeding for you. It would not do to get too familiar with a commoner, in my case more common than most.

Back in 1953, when I was 5 years old, I watched her coronation on the telly in England. The television set was of a primitive type — black and white, of course, and possibly steam-driven. It looked like a piece of alien furniture. In our innocence, we did not know yet that this alien invader would soon conquer the world to the detriment of civilization.

My old dad was working for the Reuters news agency in London, and I can only assume that my parents were not invited to the coronation due to some administrative error. The equerry probably forgot to order the third footman to inform the protocol officer at Buckingham Palace. My parents seemed to take the snub quite well.

I don't remember much from my early time in London, but I do remember the queen being crowned.

We lived in a suburb called New Malden. Up the road was a bomb crater left courtesy of the Luftwaffe. For a little kid, that crater was the coolest thing about New Malden.

I remember one other thing. Dad called from his office one evening to say he was coming home. My older brother Jim got on the phone and said: "Daddy, will you bring the papers home?" Not wishing to be left out, I naturally said: "Daddy, I want some papers too."

BACK iN 1953, *when I was 5 years old, I watched her coronation on the telly in England. The television set was of a primitive type — black and white, of course, and possibly steam-driven. It looked like a piece of alien furniture. In our innocence, we did not know yet that this alien invader would soon conquer the world to the detriment of civilization.*

I was a budding artist and could hardly wait to get my crayons and draw on paper a picture of New Malden being bombed by the Germans. But to my surprise, Dad brought home not that sort of paper but newspapers like the Daily Express and The Daily Mail. This experience changed my life. I budded in a different direction and you poor readers now suffer the consequences.

My next encounter with the monarch was 10 years later. At least I think so. By then, we had gone to Brisbane, Australia, to live — in the state of Queensland, no less. It was the custom for visiting royals to go to a local stadium for a spontaneous greeting from the city's children, spontaneous meaning forced and compulsory in this context.

Queen Elizabeth and Phillip, the Duke of Edinburgh, did make one of their royal tours Down Under in 1963, my first year of high school. But in truth, it is hard to remember clearly whether I saw Her Majesty and His Philship or one of their many relatives. All I know is that with the tropical sun beating down on us, the whole school was force-marched down to the stadium in a re-enactment of the Bataan Death March. Nothing like dehydration to warp the memory.

The next time I saw Her Majesty was when I was living in London myself, another decade on. I happened to be visiting Westminster Abbey on the very day that the queen was giving alms to needy subjects in an ancient ceremony marking Maundy Thursday. She whizzed by in her limousine, not even giving me time to yell, "Hey, Your High Highness, I'm needy too!"

The last time I saw the queen was in 1977 on the occasion of her Silver Jubilee, marking the 25th anniversary of her accession to the throne. I knew we had to stop meeting like this, because those terrible English tabloids would start talking. By then, I was working on the sports desk of The Times of London, the grand duchess of English newspapers.

We stood in Fleet Street, the heart of the newspaper business where once my old dad had worked and occupied many a bar stool, and saw the stately parade of the jubilee pass by. I had a little child on my shoulders — not my child but a child I was helping because she couldn't see, thanks to all the English people in the front who had been eating fish and chips and lard sandwiches.

The queen's gilded coach came by, not 10 feet away. Her Maj smiled and waved graciously, but not a hint of recognition was in her eyes when she saw me. It must have been the kid grabbing my hair (hey, kid, I still want it back). Yes, that must have been the reason. Hip, hip, hooray anyway. ✤

ARRGH! IT'S A PIRATE'S LIFE FOR ME

Column, Nov. 14, 2012

It's time for a confession: I have become a pirate. Arrgh, as they say in buccaneer circles. For the purposes of this column, you may call me Jamaica Jim, for that be my name.

Hurrah for pirates! They prove that when it comes to wealth redistribution, the private sector can outperform the government. Who wouldn't want to raise the black flag and sail off to adventure?

My only regret is that I am but a theatrical pirate, part of a crew of salty players assembled to navigate the biannual musical at the Edgeworth Club staged as a fundraiser by the Child Health Association of Sewickley, a charity that has been devoted to helping children since 1923.

Some may remember that I wrote about the play four years ago when I wore feathers and tights in the role of Bird No. 3. My lines then consisted of saying the single word "yeah" several times.

Still, the critics were unanimous that I had conveyed a new understanding of the natural world despite no obvious acting talent. That led to a bigger part two years ago when I was grumpy wedding tent rental guy who scowled his way through about three or four lines.

Having paid my dues, I am proud to say that I am now trusted to speak a whopping eight times, almost a nonstop babbling by my standards. Not to boast, but at this rate of progress, I'll be playing Hamlet in 100 years.

There is something wild and free about pirates, and not just in their lack of personal hygiene. As the script says, "There's a pirate that lives inside every man, and there are times when ye must be tapping into that inner pirate."

Aye, ye must! To heck with worrying about getting that book CD back to the library on time.

It seemed to me that I was a natural to be a pirate because 1) I have an accent easily adapted for pirate-talk purposes, 2) the part calls for being drunk and disorderly and, while I know nothing of that, I am willing to learn, 3) I have long been in the habit of calling non-pirates "matie" in various social situations, 4) I like to say "arrgh" because it helps to clear the bronchial tubes and 5) I am on good terms with parrots.

The producer is Marguerite Park and she also wrote the play, which is titled "A Pirate's Life for Me."

The plot concerns pirates who come to the quaint river village of Sewickley, Pa., in colonial times in a search of a treasure map (of course!). The sedate and proper townsfolk fear outbreaks of vile and unspeakable behavior, such as pirates talking with their mouths full and using the wrong fork at dinner parties.

Silly dances and romance ensue.

THERE IS SOMETHING WILD and free about pirates, and not just in their lack of personal hygiene. As the script says, "There's a pirate that lives inside every man, and there are times when ye must be tapping into that inner pirate. Aye, ye must! To heck with worrying about getting that book CD back to the library on time.

Young Marguerite is petite but has a voice of command that buckles the swash and shivers the timbers of the 35-person cast, including large and lumbering pretend pirates. Her dad is in the cast, too, and while he does a wonderful job as Marly, pirate captain, she complains that he pulls weird faces. I am too busy pulling my own weird faces to confirm the truth of this.

Indeed, we who act before the mast are Marguerite's greatest despair. Apparently, we have no talent for clumping, thus making for a messy stage with pirates wandering around like Farmer Brown's cows instead of being in neat, tight little groups.

I am not too fond of clumping myself, as I am not one of those touchy-feely buccaneers. I also have a tendency to sail off to unapproved compass points during the action. During rehearsals, Marguerite sometimes has had to come up on the stage and push me to my proper moorings. I have offered to wear roller skates to make her job easier.

My favorite scene takes place in a tavern where I am entertaining a pretty dancing girl on my lap when another lovely dancing girl pulls me away because I am so darn attractive. This is perhaps the most unlikely event in the play.

We are practicing hard for soon we will be under full sail playing before audiences for a three-night run. I want to do well for my talented fellow cast members and our invaluable support team, including Amy Jackson the choreographer and Nina Mascio, our keyboardist.

Nothing tightens the bonds of friendship more than saying arrgh for many hours together. As Gunpowder Gil, a fellow pirate, has advised me, if in doubt, say arrgh; if still in doubt, clump and say arrgh.

So I shall, for it's a pirate's life for me. Arrgh! ✱

POPE SHOWS
HOW TO BOW OUT GRACEFULLY

Column, Feb. 13, 2013

Pope Benedict XVI has decided to retire. In doing so, he has set a good example for everybody with silver hair in various strands of thinning.

Before we proceed further, a reader advisory: Those of you looking for a column critical of the pope or his church should go elsewhere. My mother was Catholic, and the church was a great solace to her all her life.

Goodness knows, both church and pope have had their problems in recent years but, out of respect for Mum, my intention today is to send good wishes to the Holy Father on a decision sensibly made. However, out of respect for Dad, who was a Protestant, I will note that the idea of an Old Popes Home is fairly hilarious no matter what denomination you are in.

But make no mistake: Pope Benedict is doing the right thing in becoming the first pope to retire in nearly 600 years. There comes a time when you just have to put the old mitre down and lift the fancy slippers up.

In the job description of pope, it clearly states that the pontiff must speak up for eternal truths — and the idea that 85 is the new 75 is not one of them. Anyone who says different should go to confession and be made to say three Hail Marys.

I appreciate the pope's leadership in promoting timely retirement. One of these days I am going to retire, too, but for the moment my mind and body are still up to the task of amusing those who like to be amused and irritating those who deserve to be irritated. Of course, I am no pontiff but I do pontificate a lot, so perhaps I can offer a few observations and timely words of advice.

Pope Benedict has announced that he will leave at 8 p.m. Feb. 28 — an unusually precise time. See, this is why I am not pope: I would have stayed around until 10 p.m., so at least I could be sure of getting a good dinner out of it before I left.

According to published reports, Pope Benedict will live in Castel Gandolfo, the papal summer retreat, after he resigns, and later move to a monastery inside the Vatican gardens. This is all good — and it avoids some elementary mistakes that regular people make all the time after retiring.

The pope has managed to avoid one of the biggest pitfalls, which is retirement in Florida. Nothing against Florida, but it can be as hot as Hades in summer. While this may present an interesting theological reminder, the sticky weather comes with the temptation to wear shorts, always to be avoided by senior church leaders, active or retired.

But a greater danger lurks in Florida — and I am not talking about the crowds of seniors filling the Winn-Dixie parking lot and leaving no space for a Popemobile. No, it's the notorious casserole ladies. These are ladies of a certain age, now single, who still like the company of men and wish to tempt new male arrivals into relationships with the aid of casseroles. Florida is no country for old popes.

As regards the aforementioned Old Popes Home, a monastery in Rome wouldn't be such a thing, of course, unless the Vatican accountants get to thinking about how to cut costs by adding more guests. This might happen naturally with other popes following the example of Pope Benedict and taking early retirement. Then several popes could get together to play checkers and complain about modern liturgical music.

But more likely, the bean counters would suggest adding some retired senior leaders from other faiths — a Coptic pope here, a grand mufti there, perhaps an archbishop of Canterbury or a televangelist. It would be very ecumenical, but it wouldn't be the same. At that stage Pope Benedict would be forgiven if he took his chances with the casserole ladies.

My concern is that like any retiree the pope might fall into unproductive elderly habits, such as playing golf, circulating reactionary emails about politicians and watching sports endlessly on TV. The pope needs to be sure to keep up his exercise and not become a pew potato. To that end, he would be well advised to take one of his encyclicals and ride it around the park every now and then.

I sincerely hope Pope Benedict has a quiet, peaceful and holy retirement, free at last from his grave responsibilities and spared the rank scribblings of certain cartoonists — you know who you are — who have made him appear like a manic raccoon about to descend on the bins.

Love him or hate him, he has earned his rest and our respect. ✳

THE POPE

has managed to avoid one of the biggest pitfalls, which is retirement in Florida. Nothing against Florida, but it can be as hot as Hades in summer. While this may present an interesting theological reminder, the sticky weather comes with the temptation to wear shorts, always to be avoided by senior church leaders, active or retired.

CHAPTER TWO

DOGS AND OTHER CRITTERS

IN DOGGED PURSUIT OF THE MASTER EDITORIAL

Column, Sept. 9, 2003

As part of a college editorial writing course I am teaching this fall, I have been reading a collection of newspaper
opinion masterpieces that have transcended their humble
fish-wrapper origins.

Inexplicably, none of my own work has been included
in the textbook "Great Editorials" (by Wm. David Sloan,
Cheryl S. Wray and C. Joanne Sloan). Despite this startling
omission, many memorable editorials are offered, including

"Is There a Santa Claus?" by Francis P. Church of the New York Sun in 1897.

Yes, Virginia, there is a Santa Claus, and there is also despair in the human heart, at least for those of us who toil in the editorial vineyards in the sure knowledge that everything we write will one day be forgotten but a guy who wrote about Santa Claus will remain an immortal. Not that I am bitter.

Another editorial that teaches humility to editorial scribblers is "Where to Bury a Dog," which was written by Ben Hur Lampman (now, there's a byline!) for The Oregonian on Sept. 11, 1925. (Note the now startling date — it was an era still innocent enough that the passing of pets was a prime subject on such a day).

This editorial is still much-beloved by dog lovers, who are a good group for a writer to have on his side. People who keep pets often take on their attributes, and so dog lovers tend to be a faithful bunch, although without the wet noses. They see a good piece in the paper, they howl. They would wag their tails if they had any.

Lampman, apparently wishing to spread the good cheer and give equal time to the cat community, also wrote an editorial titled "The Cat Can't Come Back," about what it is like to live in a house when the cat has gone off to scratch the great curtains in the sky. Whether this set the cat fanciers to purring, I don't know, but my guess is that this editorial was received with more fickleness than the dog editorial.

Like many editorial writers today, I have no claim on greatness because obviously my subject matter is too boring. In my case, away from the weekly holiday that is this column, my skills are employed in writing serious and somber pieces about medical malpractice insurance, municipal controversies and the like — in short, all proven room-emptiers.

So today, inspired by the example of Ben Hur Lampman, and in a late bid for immortality, I wish to tell you about dearly departed Lex.

Lex was a good dog, part Labrador and all goodness. Yes, yes, I know people are forever saying, "Rover, you're a good dog!" because they can't think of anything else to say to dogs, who, after all, don't know anything about the international situation or the latest trends in the art world.

But Lex was a good dog, even by the reckoning of people not short of ideas for canine conversation.

To know Lex, one must know his owner, Beth, who likes to joke that her children and friends are "perfect in every way" when we all know that she is the perfect one. She is the sort of person who cheers you up just to see her. She is kind-hearted and loyal. She is a good mother and a Steelers fan. In short, she fits all the major criteria for perfection.

Lex absorbed these lessons well, because a good person cannot have a bad dog. For 15 years, Lex was a faithful hound, a mentor to the younger pups that came into the house. But in the spring there came a sad day when Lex, now ancient in dog years, had to make a last trip to the vet's office, with tearful Beth beside him. And so to the question: Where do you bury a dog?

Late in July, my wife and I went up to Maine to stay the weekend with Beth and her husband in their cottage beside a river. The first morning Beth said, "Will you come down to the water's edge so we can deposit Lex's ashes?"

I had never been to a dog's funeral and did not know the protocol. An absurd moment occurred: Not wishing to offend, and wishing to do something, anything, I spontaneously took off my baseball cap as a mark of respect.

I HAD NEVER BEEN TO A DOG'S FUNERAL

and did not know the protocol. An absurd moment occurred: Not wishing to offend, and wishing to do something, anything, I spontaneously took off my baseball cap as a mark of respect.

Fortunately, Beth appreciated the gesture, because, being perfect in every way, she appreciates sincerity even when it is totally goofy.

So we watched Lex's few ashes disappear on the tide out to sea where the dogfish play, and I thought then of what Ben Hur Lampman had so wisely written: "The one best place to bury a good dog is in the heart of its master." ✿

GOOD DOG, SANDY

Column, July 19, 2005

Here in the dog days of summer, so named because people are hot and some tend to slobber, it is appropriate to revisit an old character who will be familiar to the faithful hounds who follow this column: my own Sandy the Wonder Dog.

It is a long time since I have mentioned Sandy, and for good reason. In recent years, the expression "let sleeping dogs lie" was made for him. He would just sit around, occasionally lifting his wizened head to snort (in canine language): "These young dogs today — they know nothing about chasing cats!"

This sedentary lifestyle wasn't too surprising. Sandy was originally dubbed a wonder dog because it was a wonder he was still breathing, considering that his life was usually poetry in non-motion. But in recent years, he raised inertia to a new and wondrous level.

Dog years had done their worst. The concept of dog years — the idea that dogs age faster than human beings — is an interesting one.

In a small way, we humans have our own variants of dog years. People grow old before their time in endless office meetings — a phenomenon known as corporate years. Another source of aging is political years — which involves listening obsessively to talk radio until the brain atrophies.

Sandy was rich in dog years. We got him in California as a young stray about 14 years ago in human terms. He was a mixed yellow lab and was named for the color of his coat.

He was a good-natured dog but never an easy one. His early months as a homeless dog had left him with a connoisseur's taste for garbage or any food left on a table. When he was young and frisky, he could sniff out a free meal at 100 paces, and he could stand up and reach for almost anything.

He once ate a frozen duck — still inside its package — that had been left out to defrost for Christmas dinner, a caper that left him in the veterinary hospital and diminished our seasonal cheer, especially when the bill arrived.

We began to live like those campers in wild places who put their food in the trees so that the bears won't devour it. But just keeping the food above the high-dog level was not enough. Sandy developed another strategy.

It is not true that old dogs can't learn new tricks. While Sandy did not join other dogs in a project to build a spaceship to put a dog on the moon before a cat could get there, he did learn how to pull a cupboard knob with his teeth, thus gaining entrance to our bread supply. Many is the time I wanted to enjoy the common luxury of toast only to find that Sandy had beaten me by a nose.

There were times when Sandy would wake from his reverie for old times' sake. He loved to go on walks and I would take him up to Sewickley Heights Park every weekend and around the block every night, rain or shine. He moved very slowly, sniffing every possible thing, until I got to pleading with him in ridiculous terms that might be called doggerel.

He also escaped from time to time, when some clown (often me) would leave a gate or a door open. Just last month, he was arrested by the local police and rode home in the back of a squad car. I was embarrassed, of course, but he looked very pleased with himself.

Needless to say, we grew very close to this lazy, irritating, Houdini dog who was extremely good-natured and lovable.

For my own part, I would look forward to that moment after a day at work when I would come down the garden path and see Sandy lying impassively Sphinx-like except for his big tail sweeping the floor in greeting.

Perhaps it is my personality, but very few living, breathing creatures show enthusiasm at my arrival. I am not sure my wife would wag her tail if she had one.

That is why they call dogs like Sandy Man's Best Friend, even if they do steal the bread. They have been like this ever since they first came to our camp fires 10,000 years ago.

And ever since then, we humans have dreaded the inevitable day that comes when those dog years outstrip our own. You realized — didn't you? — that I have been writing in the past tense. Last week, we took Sandy, old and sick and feeble, for his final ride. He slipped away very quietly, with his paws out front and his nose on the floor, the Sphinx gone to join the ages.

IT IS NOT TRUE

that old dogs can't learn new tricks. While Sandy did not join other dogs in a project to build a spaceship to put a dog on the moon before a cat could get there, he did learn how to pull a cupboard knob with his teeth, thus gaining entrance to our bread supply.

I come home now and half expect to see the friendly sweeping tail. I think to hide the food at a higher elevation but sadly have to check myself. I want to walk through the back alley at midnight, but can't because the police take a dim view of it. And I eat my toast with no appetite, because the joy of finding the bread intact is no longer mine. ✱

HIS BILLS ARE WORSE
THAN HIS BITE

Column, Sept. 27, 2005

Back in July, I wrote a column about Sandy the Wonder Dog, my four-legged companion who went to his final reward after a distinguished life of getting into the breadbox and otherwise lying around doing nothing.

It was my intention to have a decent period of mourning for Sandy. But my daughter, Allison, came home from her summer job and immediately declared: "This family needs a dog." This was in the finest tradition of her mother, who holds that while the position of man of the house is theoretically occupied, it's not as if his opinions count for anything.

Allison had no definite plan for dog procurement, but in our local village she found a clothing store — SoHo of Sewickley — whose kindly owner displays pictures of animals in the window. Some are older dogs, who have been around the park several times and are suddenly displaced or need to be rescued from bad situations — their hapless owners perhaps having been impoverished by having to gas up their SUVs.

Rather than leave these situational orphans to a cruel fate, good homes are sought for them. As Allison first told me all this, little violins seemed to be playing in the background, so I assumed that this effort had an e-mail address something like arf@dogsforsuckers.com.

Then, as I was going out the door one Saturday morning on my way to hone my reputation for eccentricity (I don't wish to seem more-eccentric-than-thou but I do play cricket in my spare time), Allison and her mother informed me that they had seen a picture of a very cute dog and were going to see it. He was a black-and-white lab and spaniel mix — and only 9 years old!

Be smart, I said. Make sure you really like this dog. Ask the vital questions (e.g., does it chew expensive imported cricket bats?). Oh, they said, we won't make rash decisions. Oh no.

Of course, I left for the match thinking that, win or lose, the ever-sticky wicket of dog ownership was in my future. Now, this could have been one of those "Am I a man or a chihuahua?" moments. But it seemed like all protest was futile, so I yapped and left the house.

What consoled me was the thought that it is a good thing that deserving old dogs (and some other animals) are given a second chance.

Why, if my wife one day tires of me going to cricket matches and hands me my hat, I hope that such a service will be available for humans. Perhaps a kindly widow or divorced lady will see my picture in the dress-shop window, mistake sadness for cuteness and be impressed that I am house-trained.

During the game, at a time when nothing much was happening (and admittedly nothing happens quite a lot in cricket), I got a call on my cell phone from Allison. "Guess what, Dad?" (Hmm, I wonder what it is?) "We've got a dog!"

Of course we do. That afternoon I got to meet Sooner, as in the hit song lyric — "Sooner or later, love is going to getcha." It seems that his previous owner was disabled and Sooner had become too much of a handful.

I could see why. Sooner is the friskiest 9-year-old dog in the world, and he's a little powerhouse.

He is also very affectionate. It seems that he has been taught to extend his paw to everyone he meets. Ever since he arrived, I have been shaking his paw, feeling like a politician running for dog catcher.

He has some faults — don't we all? He is not good on the leash and is a bit of a bolter. Then again, I am not good on the leash either (metaphorical, in my case), so I can't hold that against him.

SOONER IS THE FRISKIEST

9-year-old dog in the world, and he's a little powerhouse. He is also very affectionate. It seems that he has been taught to extend his paw to everyone he meets. Ever since he arrived, I have been shaking his paw, feeling like a politician running for dog catcher.

A complimentary set of fleas came with him. Between the flea remedies, a new hidden electric fence for the yard, a veterinarian check-up and various shots, we have an answer to the eternal question: "How much is that doggie in the window?" Turns out that "almost free" is going on several hundreds of dollars.

But this was to be expected, according to the Reg Henry Theorem of Life No. 632, which states: "Everybody we love in life costs us a fortune in love and exasperation." It's not cricket, but sooner or later... ✱

NAMES FOR ALL CREATURES GREAT AND SMALL

Column, Oct. 7, 2009

When my old friend Doug came over from Australia to see the sights in America, including the inside of my fridge where the beer is kept, he was much taken with the abundance of squirrels in the area.

As he had never seen such a thing, he coined a term for the multiple squirrels that congregated on the lawn — a *thanat* of squirrels. Why he chose "thanat" for squirrel groupings I can't really say, but possibly he derived it from the Greek word *thanatos,* meaning death.

While this doesn't make much sense at first blush, it might seem more fitting if you were a plump nut or acorn and a hungry squirrel were approaching — and no offense to you plump nuts; I'm a bit pudgy myself.

On other hand, my mate Doug may have just made up *thanat* after a few drinks. Still, his name for a squirrel congregation certainly was in the long tradition of fancy animal-group monikers, such as a *pride* of lions — a piece of big-cat egotism that always gives the hyenas a laugh (a *cackle* of hyenas, by the way.)

Lists of animal group names are available on the Web and they make great reading if you happen to have some spare time on your hands, say, on death row waiting to be executed, or in a newspaper waiting for the industry to be executed.

Pretty much every animal has a group name except apparently groundhogs, which is a shocking omission that I hereby rectify by suggesting a *prognostication* of groundhogs in honor of the famous meteorologist Punxsutawney Phil.

Some of my favorite animal group names are a *murder* of crows (surely a homicide of crows, those crows haven't been convicted yet) and a *business* of ferrets (what business ferrets engage in is anyone's guess, but I'm thinking telemarketing).

Yes, some of these names are doozies and, until I read them again, I did not realize that squirrels already had a group name — a *scurry* or a *dray* of squirrels.

I can understand scurry — it is totally descriptive — but dray? A dray is a low, sturdy cart with detachable sides. You couldn't haul a load of squirrels in a dray; they'd be over the top or through the detachable sides in no time.

So, as it turns out, *thanat* is free to be applied to other groupings and I think it is past time to use colorfully descriptive names for human beings who deserve them more. Really, what have these animals done that we have to call them names? Because giraffes are tall, we have to call them *a tower* of giraffes? Oh, yeah, make fun of giraffes, just because they stick their necks out.

It is not fair. Take for example, the name for bears in a group — a *sleuth* or *sloth* of bears. That name is wasted on the bears. It would be better if "sleuth" were applied to groups of detectives and "sloth" to employees of certain state agencies.

PRETTY MUCH EVERY ANIMAL

has a group name except apparently groundhogs, which is a shocking omission that I hereby rectify by suggesting a prognostication of groundhogs in honor of the famous meteorologist Punxsutawney Phil.

Then there's *a bloat* of hippopotamuses, which is really quite insulting to full-figured hippopotami, who can look quite nice if they put flowers in their ears and become (old joke alert) hippypotamuses. Much better, I think, to apply *bloat* to Americans in general.

As for those of you who are more petite and do not deserve to be counted in the bloat, please do not feel left out. There are words enough to describe your group classification. A *misery* of dieters. A *sweat* of joggers. A *stretch* of yoga enthusiasts. (You can thank your lucky stars that among the *depression* of journalists, there is one still thinking of such important topics.)

Where we Americans are most lacking is in names for our political groupings. We live in an era when many conservatives are un-conservative and many liberals are illiberal and at least these strange political groups should have names of their own. I suggest a *grumble* of conservatives and an *equivocation* of liberals.

These groupings may also find a home in the major political parties, where one can readily find a *naysaying* of Republicans and a *spending* of Democrats.

The tea party folks also deserve a name, something like *a fury* of tea party-goers, and the Birthers likewise — *a delusion* of birth-certificate doubters. I tell you, more strange birds live in this world than came off Noah's ark two by two.

But what to do about "thanat"? I have saved it until last: *A thanat* of congressional lobbyists. They are squirrelly in their ways and they are death to meaningful reform. They count their nuts and they leave the rest of us up a tree. Why, we need *a business* of ferrets to sort them out. ✳

CHAPTER THREE

HAPPiNESS IS NOT A WARM GUN

A BULL'S-EYE FOR VICE PRESIDENT CHENEY

Column, Feb. 14, 2006

Sometimes a story comes along that presents a unique chance to educate the American people. I refer, of course, to Vice President Dick Cheney shooting an attorney.

Several knee-jerk reactions to this news must be countered immediately. First of all, Mr. Cheney should not be hailed as a popular hero for bagging a lawyer. People, even attorneys, are always out of season, even in Texas. Besides, they often shoot back with writs, and nothing spoils a hunt more than the quarry turning on the hunter with a hail of lawsuits, known to be more deadly than birdshot.

The other thing is that attorneys do not make good eating. The one that Mr. Cheney shot was a tough old bird and is already sitting up and taking nourishment. Even cannibals won't touch attorneys because they are so hard-boiled.

Knees will also jerk in the opposite direction. In effete circles where guns are not appreciated, this incident will make an easy target for criticism. Let me just remind these anti-gun critics that guns don't wound people, vice presidents wound people.

Nor should this be an occasion for piling on Mr. Cheney. He is an avid hunter who blasts away at birds at every opportunity, protecting the nation from avian flu, something for which he gets no credit.

Given the number of shots he takes, he is bound to hit an attorney from time to time because they are very thick on the ground here in America, and it's simply a matter of mathematical probability. Anybody could have made the same mistake.

One of my regular readers e-mailed me to make an important point: When John Kerry went hunting during the presidential campaign, conservatives maligned him as a poseur — and he didn't even shoot anybody!

It does seem unfair, but that was part of Sen. Kerry's problem. Rightly or wrongly, the American public thought he was the sort of guy you couldn't trust to wing anybody at a law firm picnic.

The real lesson to be drawn here is about firearm safety. The war on terror is going to last a very long time — it has to, because more Republicans have to be elected. This means that we are all going to have to familiarize ourselves with firearms to protect the homeland.

As it happens, I can help. I was trained on many weapons for my military service in Vietnam — the rifle, the machine gun, the hand grenade, the typewriter and the can opener.

Mr. Cheney did not go to Vietnam. If the VC had worn duck suits instead of black pajamas, he would have been the first to enlist. But he decided to leave the job to people like myself, which may explain why his firearm handling leaves something to be desired.

The cardinal rule of firearms is that you don't shoot until you have properly identified the target. Don't shoot until you see the whites of their eyes! Of course, if the person you are shooting has had a night on the town and has bloodshot eyes, you are in for trouble. That is why in Vietnam we were told: "Don't shoot until you see the red of their politics!"

In this incident, Mr. Cheney — perhaps due to faulty intelligence — did not stop and distinguish between quail and attorney before he started shooting. Quail are said to congregate in a covey whereas attorneys flock together in what is called a bar. Any decent field guide has identifying pictures to assist the hunter.

Thank goodness no serious harm was done! It's not like Mr. Cheney shot up a whole country looking for weapons of mass destruction.

IN THIS INCIDENT,

Mr. Cheney — perhaps due to faulty intelligence — did not stop and distinguish between quail and attorney before he started shooting. Quail are said to congregate in a covey whereas attorneys flock together in what is called a bar. Any decent field guide has identifying pictures to assist the hunter.

My faithful reader suggests we start a fund to buy body armor for Mr. Cheney's hunting buddies, considering the danger they are in. Yes, I know what Donald Rumsfeld would say: You go hunting with the hunting equipment you've got. But I think the vice president's pals need extra help, too, and I would suggest that we also print up bumper stickers for our cars: "Support Our Well-Connected Attorneys Before They Become Dead Ducks." ✤

RAMPANT GUN CULTURE AIDED BY COWARDICE

Column, Dec. 19, 2012

This is not the column I wanted to write. This is not the column you wanted to read. But a grim vision, the residue of dread left by a terrible day at a Connecticut elementary school, seizes the imagination.

In the mind's eye, it conjures up children's stockings and those of six brave adults, hung with care but robbed now of their Christmas joy before cold family hearths

But what is the right way to honor the needlessly dead? Not with merriment and laughter, not today. Perhaps the only way is a humble offering of a few home truths, so obvious that they are not universally grasped, so truthful that many people cannot bring themselves to believe them. As the old saying has it, none so blind as those who will not see.

The obvious starts, as it always does, with the one-word question: Why? The strange aspect of this question is that most people already instinctively know the answer. Of course, nobody knows the exact mind or motive of the shooter in Connecticut and maybe never will. But that is the least part implied by the question.

Why? Because this is America, one of the most heavily armed nations in the world. In America, guns have their venerated place next to Mom and apple pie. They have been placed on a constitutional pedestal as being indispensable to liberty itself, although people in other civilized, democratic counties are living proof that this isn't true.

Where guns are so readily available, where custom and laws insist that the gun culture is supreme, supposedly rare massacres of the innocent become both inevitable and commonplace. Every so often, a troubled person will pick up a gun and kill. That's why.

Why ask why? Do workers who slosh around in petroleum up to their knees and smoke cigarettes ask why fires start? Do lifeguards at beaches with treacherous undertows ask why swimmers drown?

We know why. It's the guns, and not just any guns but guns that fire more rounds in quicker time than the musket-toting Founding Fathers ever dreamed of when writing the Second Amendment.

Do we think that the writers of the Constitution, if they knew what we now know, would have proceeded as they did? And if we do think so, what do we really believe about those wise gentlemen — that they lacked compassion or brains?

Yet some Americans say that the answer to gun violence is more guns, as if the answer to petroleum fires is more petroleum and more smoking. They would take America back to the Wild West, everyone armed from Miss Kitty to Marshal Dillon, the schoolmarm and her pupils, with the local undertaker doing a roaring business amid the clouds of gun smoke, and all in the name of safety.

This is nuts, but it is also ignorant of human nature. It assumes that everybody can be turned into effective killers just by giving them guns. Most people, even when threatened in an emergency, could not be depended upon to take someone's else's life — and thank God for our natures.

This is why the military puts its recruits through weeks of rigourous boot camp, not just to make them fit and familiar with weapons, but to break down the fundamental human inhibitions against killing. Psychopaths find killing easy, normal people have to be trained how to overcome their normal social impulses.

Americans may be stuck with the Second Amendment as a permanent artifact of history, but there's much we could do to read it sensibly and enforce it wisely.

The Second Amendment is not absolute; no amendment is, including the First Amendment. The reach of all amendments stretches no farther than the point where they intrude on other rights. All the child and adult victims in Newtown were criminally deprived of all their constitutional rights because of one, the Second Amendment, which made high-powered guns available for the slaughter. That is just wrong. That is just stupid.

The American people find themselves doomed to relive a tale from Greek mythology, the one in which the Athenians periodically send seven boys and seven girls as tribute to a Cretan king. There they are fed to the minotaur, a half-bull, half-man monster, who lives in a labyrinth. Finally, the hero Theseus slays the beast in its lair.

YET SOME AMERICANS

say that the answer to gun violence is more guns, as if the answer to petroleum fires is more petroleum and more smoking. They would take America back to the Wild West, everyone armed from Miss Kitty to Marshal Dillon, the schoolmarm and her pupils, with the local undertaker doing a roaring business amid the clouds of gun smoke, and all in the name of safety.

We are not at that part of the story yet, just the part where we regularly sacrifice our youth in a labyrinth of excuses. Where is our hero among coward politician kings and their unthinking supporters?

Every time someone says that we don't need more gun laws but we need more guns, the minotaur grows stronger. Why? In God's name, why? ✸

A LACK OF LOGIC ON GUNS KILLS PEOPLE

Column, Jan. 16, 2013

As you know, cookies don't fatten people, people fatten themselves by eating cookies — and if that makes any sense to you, congratulations, because you have won a prize. To claim the prize, just pull my other leg and wait until you hear the bell ring. An operator will assist you.

The arguments against gun control are a bit like that — much puzzling nonsense and a long wait before anything happens if it happens at all.

While the Obama administration figures out how to proceed with sensible rules on gun purchases that will take America from being armed to the teeth to being armed only to the elbows, let us look at a couple of the major obstacles to the cause of sanity.

The biggest is a strange and disturbing twist on patriotism: Those who love their guns like little boys love their teddy bears insist that the Second Amendment is not about protecting a right to hunt, say, but the means of resisting government tyranny. The precise moment they say this is when they leave the real United States behind in the rearview mirror and enter the realm of Crazyland.

Consider the irony: Every self-professed patriot becomes teary-eyed about the flag and those whose job it is to fight to protect it — and rightly so. By and large, members of the Armed Forces today are widely admired and respected.

But if guns were used in an effort to overthrow a tyrannical government, guess who the enemy would be? Why, those same men and women of the Armed Forces marching under that same grand old flag. The president, if a reminder is needed, is their commander in chief.

Count me out. The idea is totally repugnant. Tyranny, you say? People who raise the threat of government tyranny should be congratulated — but only for having lived a sheltered life. North Korea is a tyranny, the old Soviet Union was a tyranny, the United States is not a tyranny, not even close, not under Barack Obama. not previously under George W. Bush.

Like everything in modern life, the word "tyrant" has been devalued and dumbed down to the point of meaninglessness. What we have is a government that some people don't like — and fair enough, they may have good reason. It was ever thus: Abraham Lincoln was considered a tyrant but he left words to describe what we really do have, however imperfectly, "a government of the people, by the people and for the people."

Any American who needs an assault weapon for possibly making war on his supposedly dictatorial government is really contemplating another Civil War. Has the nation become so brain-dead that it has forgotten the horrors of brother fighting brother? At least the Civil War was about real issues, not the sour fruit of paranoia that makes some of today's alleged patriots so dyspeptic.

If the Second Amendment was really about empowering the people to resist despotism, why doesn't it allow everybody to have machine guns and rocket-propelled grenades the better to succeed in their resistance? Because even the most right-wing judges in the land are not that crazy.

Besides, the idea that the Founding Fathers were almost inviting armed insurrection with the Second Amendment does not square with the historical record. Not long after the Revolution, farmers in Western Pennsylvania rose up violently to oppose a tax on the whiskey they distilled from their grain (they wanted to become excited about something but the Steelers had yet to be invented).

The Whiskey Rebellion was put down in 1794 by an army sent by President George Washington, who rode at the head of it. From the earliest, the federal government made it clear that it wasn't going to tolerate any nonsense from armed blowhards who thought freedom meant anarchy.

We should take the point. Gun extremists shouldn't be allowed to justify possession of hugely powerful guns that can massacre a crowd of kids quickly and efficiently because those guns might one day be needed to be turned on the government to preserve freedom. At this point of our bloody history, this should not be a respectable idea. There is an old word that we should resurrect for this poisonous argument: Treasonous.

Indeed, if you think you must have an assault rifle to fight your own government and people, you might as well think about joining al-Qaida and have done with it. I understand that if you join this month, you get a T-shirt and a complimentary bag of dates.

...IF YOU THINK *you must have an assault rifle to fight your own government and people, you might as well think about joining al-Qaida and have done with it. I understand that if you join this month, you get a T-shirt and a complimentary bag of dates.*

Guns don't kill people? What are certain guns but killing machines? Killing machines made by people to kill other people. The real prize goes to those who can think their way to reducing the carnage. ✸

CHAPTER FOUR

THIS SPORTING LIFE

PADDLE TENNIS CAN THWACK A MALE EGO AND MAKE MEN HEEL

Column, March 2, 1999

Everybody has heard of Punxsutawney Phil, the weather woodchuck, but few know of Sewickley Sam, the golden retriever who in February looks out over his estate and predicts six more weeks of paddle tennis.

Yes, paddle tennis. As they observe ruefully in certain Pittsburgh circles, it's the only known way to keep the cake-eating classes confined in a cage.

If you have not seen the game, it is like a miniature version of tennis played outside in the winter months with a rubber ball. The racket is a rigid, oval-shaped paddle and the court is on an elevated platform enclosed by wire.

It is sometimes called platform tennis, or, more simply, "that darn game."

As it happens, I live deep in the heart of paddle country, where the plop, plop of balls on paddles measures the hours like a grandfather clock and the thwack, thwack of the ball coming off the wire is as sexy to local ears as the snapping of thong underwear is to our president.

Women, in particular, are notoriously fanatical about the game. In fact, women are not allowed to live in certain suburbs unless they play. The game is taken so seriously that the politics of women's paddle tennis always threaten to require NATO intervention.

Because these ladies spend so many hours practicing, they can play on almost equal terms to men, who for the most part simply rely on the traditional male attributes of strength and charm, the latter attribute not always acknowledged.

This past weekend, one of the most venerable local mixed tournaments was held once again - the Sewickley Invitational Paddle Tournament (SIPT). For more than 30 years, local players have invited out-of-town guests who apparently are in desperate need of amusement.

For example, my wife had two sisters, their husbands and her brother playing, and, of course, I took part as well, because, hey, it would not have looked good if I had stayed lurking in the cozy hut out of the rain and all the fun.

At the highest level, paddle tennis is a game of finesse and patience. Each point can go on for a great length of time, sometimes focused on just one player forced back into a corner, bravely returning impossible shots off the wire while his partner either watches anxiously or reads the newspaper.

This is not my level. In the SIPT, I am always in the last of three flights - the "Abandon Hope All Yea Who Enter Here" division. At this level, if the ball crosses the net half a dozen times, the astonished players become giddy with excitement and stop and congratulate each other.

Not surprisingly, I did not win the flight or any of the consolation finals. As always, I ended up an M.L. - or Male Loser, as the program so charmingly designates us.

This was my own fault, of course, and I wish to apologize to my partners who were models of cheerfulness and support. The fact is that I am the Jubilation T. Cornpone of paddle tennis, that gallant soldier in the L'il Abner musical of long ago who was forever pulling defeat from the jaws of victory.

But the way I look at it, if I were really good at paddle tennis, would it not be the final sign of a wasted life? Isn't it enough that I write a silly column once a week? Besides, there are Male Losers and there are Male Losers.

Consider my brother-in-law Nat, a natural athlete and gentleman. When I drove him to the Sewickley YMCA courts for his game in a higher flight, I pointed out Sewickley Valley

WOMEN, IN PARTICULAR, *are notoriously fanatical about the game. In fact, women are not allowed to live in certain suburbs unless they play. The game is taken so seriously that the politics of women's paddle tennis always threaten to require NATO intervention.*

Hospital across the road. "That's really convenient," he said. "I can go over there when I have my heart attack."

With an hour, he was over there, being examined not for a heart attack but a severed Achilles tendon. Ouch! Well, that's what you get for moving about the court, which personally I always try to avoid.

At least Nat was in no danger of dying of nurture. His sisters, being paddle-playing women, are impressively tough. "Let this be a lesson to you, Nat, for being so out of shape," they said in chorus. Then his wife grabbed the crutches and demonstrated how ridiculous he looked coming out of the hospital. "In any other family, you would be treated with sympathy," he observed. "In this family, they do skits about you."

Ah, life in the suburbs, where men are men and women play paddle tennis, and spring can't come soon enough after the dog days of winter. ✱

ALL AT SEA
AMONG THE SAILING SET

Column, Aug. 20, 2002

Avast there, me hearties. Tie your vessel to a handy mooring and listen to a tale of the high seas from a salty-dog correspondent.

The first chapter of this adventure starts when my brother-in-law — let us call him Captain Michael — takes his new 31-foot motor boat for a little spin up the East branch of the Westport (Mass.) River at a bracing 20 knots.

As it is low tide, it doesn't seem to me to be the smartest maneuver in the annals of navigation, but what do I know? I am not the captain, just the mate (being originally from Australia, I am always the mate).

Ever attentive to my duties, I am having a little nap on the couch at the stern, the better to be prepared to spring into action.

But then we hit the sandbar that mysteriously appears in the middle of the channel — so it isn't necessary for me to spring up, because my body is thrown through the air, performing several involuntary pirouettes before landing in a heap on the deck.

It suddenly occurs to me why sailors swear so much, but there is no time for further thoughts. Captain Michael orders all hands overboard to try to push the boat off the sandbar. Meanwhile, he stays nice and dry at the helm, giving contradictory orders.

To add to the fun, the riverbed consists of primeval ooze and those pushing the boat begin to sink into it.

Just in time, a cheerful thought comes to mind that I share with my shipmates. "We should count our blessings, lads. The boat is not completely wrecked. And although I am black and blue, and my bleeding threatens to attract sharks or even prehistoric sea monsters hibernating in the muck, at least our spouses won't find out about this debacle."

BUT THEN WE HIT THE SANDBAR

that mysteriously appears in the middle of the channel — so it isn't necessary for me to spring up, because my body is thrown through the air, performing several involuntary pirouettes before landing in a heap on the deck.

No sooner had these fateful words been spoken, than two familiar-looking women paddle up in kayaks. "Yoo hoo," they yell. "It's us. What are you doing in the water?"

But that was last summer. Would more adventures befall Captain Michael and his merry crew of amateur mariners this year? Well, of course.

This year, however, everybody had learned their lessons. Captain Michael himself has become quite the seafaring man. Why, he ran aground only once, and he wasn't even going very fast and nobody was injured. Always one to give credit when it is due, I told him: "You are flirting with competence."

As for me, I was determined to be a model crew member. To that end, I listened intently as another brother-in-law, Nat, who actually knows something about boats, gave us all a lesson in tying the bowline. "You make a loop," he said, "then you imagine a monkey coming up the hole and around the tree ...."

While I never mastered this knot, I did learn a lot about monkeys.

But the greatest test was to come — and, with all due modesty, I came through magnificently, although this is not a unanimous opinion.

We had stopped at a yacht club pier (I won't say which one, because we want to go back) to pick up sister-in-law Janie for a harbor cruise. A small fleet of 12-meter yachts, including some of the famous old America's Cup competitors, were in port for a regatta and a couple of these beauties were moored at the end of the pier.

Janie was late, so Nat got off to look for her. The boat's engine was idling away in neutral, and Captain Michael became impatient and he also got off. I was left alone at the stern, trying not to make eye contact with assorted chaps in blazers on the dock.

Suddenly, the boat started to go backward. This couldn't be! Thinking perhaps the boat was being forced back by another boat's wake, I instinctively grabbed a pylon and hung on like that monkey going around the tree.

But that wasn't working. The boat was in reverse and gaining speed fast. Lines parted. I looked over my shoulder and saw we were heading directly for the 12-meter yachts in all their multimillion-dollar glory. In a few more seconds, we would surely collide and sink them.

Someone on the dock yelled, "Grab the throttle!"

Although largely uncertain about the controls, I leapt forward and threw the throttle forward. The boat surged ahead and settled. Disaster was averted.

None of us can figure out why it suddenly went into reverse, but, of course, Captain Michael blames me. He believes fiasco emanates from my body in ways that upset the natural order.

My reaction, maties, is that the next time we get on a sandbar, he can get out and push himself off. ✹

THE NAKED TRUTH:
DAD IS SON'S BIGGEST FAN

Column, April 29, 2003

Let me share with you today the sort of e-mail you don't want to receive from your son in college:

"Dad, I might join the ranks of the ... varsity streaking team. Wish me luck. Jimmy."

This came last week and included an e-mail sent to all students at his college, inviting them to join "the Co-ed Varsity Streaking Team" at noon the next Wednesday — this despite a forecast calling for a chance of snow in that region of upstate New York. "People of all shapes, sizes and colors are welcome," it said.

Clearly, he sent it to get me mad. He knows the last thing I need in my life is a call from campus security telling me he had been caught naked in the quadrangle.

In my view, it's no time to be naked in America. Heck, Sen. Rick Santorum sees no constitutional problem in police officers coming into your house and arresting you for having sex not approved by the government.

If the cop is to be put into copulation, my fear is that officers may crack down on streakers, with a view to making sure that the participants' dating opportunities are not boosted by their having flagrantly advertised their charms.

So I immediately rose to the bait and e-mailed him back: "Jim, Keep your pants on. We Henrys do better when we are subtle. Dad xxxx."

Of course, this advice was nonsense. This is America and subtlety is a complete loser, for Henrys or anyone else. Only people who are completely over-the-top make any impression in America (ask Sen. Santorum). But I had to write something before he threw pants and caution to the wind.

Jimmy knows his father all too well: If a varsity streaking team really existed, competing in an approved league of athletic nudists (presumably in a summer season), then I certainly would come and cheer for him, although goodness knows where he would pin his number.

No matter what sport my children played, I have always been the biggest father fan.

Now, it would be tasteless to suggest that unathletic people like me only have children so that they can beat other people's children in sporting contests, as a pathetic revenge for all the times we were picked last in childhood pick-up games.

Still, when a parent reads "Goodnight Moon" to a little kid, it is only natural to wish that one day heaven will reward such excruciating sappiness by having the child grow up and hit a game-winning home run.

My support for Jimmy started early with T-ball and swarm ball (otherwise known as soccer for 5-year-olds).

When he finally got to Little League, no parent was in the bleachers more often than I was, shouting the traditional "Good eye, good eye," when the ball sailed 10 feet over his head and he decided not to swing at it. You'd think Jimmy was Cyclops Jr., so often was he praised for having a good eye.

I thought baseball or soccer would be his game. But when we moved from California to Pittsburgh, he took up ice hockey. Oh, that was some kind of fun for me, going to games at godforsaken hours in far-flung rinks where devoted moms (most impressively) would howl in the stands and heap abuse on the poor refs.

Then he discovered a new sport at his school — lacrosse, a sort of land-based hockey invented by the American Indians. He took to it immediately, and that's no surprise. What red-blooded boy doesn't respond to being given a stick and being told he can hit people with it?

Now that he is playing lacrosse in college, I travel 400 miles to see him play every chance I get. Later, I take him to dinner, and a few friends tag along, actually about half the team, and of course they all order steaks because hitting people with sticks inspires a hearty appetite, and, hey, Jimmy's dad is buying.

No complaints. The experience is worth every penny. Jimmy plays attack, which means he must navigate through a thicket of big bruiser defensemen to score goals. The college paper recently called him the "eclectic dodger,"

JIMMY KNOWS HIS FATHER

all too well: If a varsity streaking team really existed, competing in an approved league of athletic nudists (presumably in a summer season), then I certainly would come and cheer for him, although goodness knows where he would pin his number.

because he has an amazing talent for changing direction in a twinkling — a trait he obviously inherited from his mother.

All the while, I am up in the stands, beaming with pride and saying to no one in particular: "Look, that's my son, the eclectic dodger." So it's just as well he has his shorts on as his winning streak continues. ✱

A LETTER TO MY SON
AT GAME'S END

Column, May 3, 2005

Dear Jimmy,

It is finally over. I have been following your sporting contests since you were 5 with the pride only a father with little athletic ability of his own could muster.

When you played your last college lacrosse game last week, I felt infinitely sad, not because your team lost — hey, we had them all the way except for the little matter of scoring enough goals — but because it marked another chapter in life closing with a thud.

For you, this was a good thing. For those who play lacrosse — a game in which unkindly bruisers hit you with sticks — it is a fair bet that life can only improve. Now, graduation beckons and, like the man with the wheelbarrow, everything rolls before you.

But for me it's a different story. My one foot is a little further planted in the grave, and I don't have the consolation of defying the funeral by shouting encouragement to you. I hope my presence on the sidelines wasn't an embarrassment. On occasion I embarrassed your mother, but she was under the impression that it was only a game. A game? Phooey! It was life.

And what a life it was! My only regret was that I did not go to every game, but I went to 11 of 14 down the last six-week stretch. Fortunately, Hamilton College is only 396 miles from Pittsburgh, and it would be an easy drive if it weren't for the regular blizzards and torrential rain in Erie and upstate New York.

Your Mom, of course, thought I was quite mad, and she hasn't completely forgiven me for buying her Mother's Day present last year at a truck stop on the way back from one of your games. Heck, it wasn't my fault that the lottery ticket didn't win.

Once upon a time, my Dad used to watch me play sports, but I did not give him much to cheer about. You have a special gift. That you did not get your talent from me, but from other athletic relatives, did not discourage me in the least. That is how life's mad old mating game is supposed to work. You trade genes with one you love and, if it all works out, it's the Revenge of the Nerds.

The one thing I take pride in passing on to you was a strong strategic sense. You possessed the ability to see the whole field.

In whatever I have done, I have always seen all the possibilities unfolding, too — although, in my case, I haven't been able to do anything about them. It is a good thing I did not kill myself driving up to the games. Otherwise, my epitaph might have read: "He Saw the Whole Field, but He Did Not See the Truck."

You keep your eyes open, too. It's enough that you had the distinction of being perhaps the only NCAA player to have been caught in the tsunami. I know you are thoroughly sick of being the "tsunami guy," the player who got out of the pool in Phuket just in time, but it was inspired of your coach to get fans to donate money for every goal scored this season and direct it to tsunami relief.

Yes, I know you had in mind a humanitarian keg party, but a goal-athon was the better way. As it is, between you and your great teammates, I am happily out a chunk of change.

MY ONLY REGRET

was that I did not go to every game, but I went to 11 of 14 down the last six-week stretch. Fortunately, Hamilton College is only 396 miles from Pittsburgh, and it would be an easy drive if it weren't for the regular blizzards and torrential rain in Erie and upstate New York.

You were lucky to play at the school you did. Other guys get to play for the Gophers or the Warthogs, or whatever, but you guys were the Continentals. Now there's a name!

Although the Continentals did not do as well as the famous Hamilton College Streaking Team this year, I am glad you kept your pants on. Not to take anything away from that fine body of students, so to speak, but playing lacrosse you had less chance of catching cold.

When you walked off the field last week after Union College had played Aaron Burr to Hamilton's playoff hopes, you looked up to me dejected and said: "I'm sorry, Dad." It broke my heart, for there was nothing at all to be sorry about.

Remember, son, when the great scorer marks your name, it's not that you won or lost, but how you did at the tailgate party. In my dreary post-lacrosse life, which I fear your mother has already organized, I will recall these days with joy.

Thanks, Jim. ✽

THE DOGGEDNESS OF
THE LONG-DISTANCE RUNNER

Column, Aug. 8, 2007

Each of us has his (or her) own way of combating the national obesity crisis. Some people eat a lot in the hope that they will lose weight when they finally explode. Some go on diets, because it makes them feel miserable, which they equate with being virtuous.

Given these choices, we should all be exercising instead. I recommend rolling up the newspaper and performing calisthenics with it. While it may not do much for your biceps, pectorals, deltoids or even your asteroids, it could have a very healthy effect on newspaper circulation if it catches on.

Yes, I know that exercise can be a nasty and inconvenient business. It can involve wearing tights, which many of us — in particular me — are well advised to avoid. Exercise also induces perspiration, which is not good on crowded buses. If exercise and public transportation are not mixed, however, there is no problem. After all, sweat is merely nature's way of telling us we need a bath.

As it happens, I am a toiling runner and have been one for at least 15 years. Years ago, out in California, I had a midlife crisis and began running marathons, which is really all I could do because I couldn't afford a red sports car and a blond girlfriend.

While my marathon days are over, I still call myself a runner, but I am probably more accurately called a jogger or even a plodder. I do not know the exact difference between running and jogging, but I guess it is about 5 mph — more than I can muster except when being chased by a dog. (A plodder is slower still. Dogs don't bother plodders because there is no thrill in the chase.)

I am a traditional runner in that I run through the streets like a mad person. Some people prefer to do their running on treadmills. This is good exercise, but for my part, if I want to expend a lot of energy in getting nowhere, I can always just come to work.

This is not to slight this or any other form of exercise — to each his own. Yoga has swept America in recent years and understandably so. Many people now have the ability to twist their bodies into eccentric positions, sometimes with their backsides in the air where their heads might normally be — which may explain how George W. Bush won the last presidential election.

Cycling is also great exercise and has the advantage over stationary bikes in that the touring cyclist gets to see real scenery — such as the inside of emergency rooms when he or she falls off.

While I enjoy falling off a bike as much as the next person, what really keeps me from becoming a pedaling fanatic is that I live in fear of mechanical troubles — a flat tire, a broken chain —

I AM A TRADITIONAL RUNNER

in that I run through the streets like a mad person. Some people prefer to do their running on treadmills. This is good exercise, but for my part, if I want to expend a lot of energy in getting nowhere, I can always just come to work.

that will leave me stranded in the countryside while dressed in clothing that is in the same league as tights when it comes to concerns about public decency.

No, what I like best is going for a simple, natural run. It takes no equipment except a pair of running shoes, an old T-shirt and pair of shorts.

Ever modest, I do not favor the very brief running shorts that some show-offs wear. I feel there is enough sex in our society without me inflaming passions in the borough of Sewickley. As it is, the ladies say: "Who is that handsome devil impersonating a snail? And what is he wearing: long shorts or short longs?"

What I love about running is finding unexpected sights. I am just back from a vacation in Westport, Mass., which is very close to the Rhode Island line. I ate, I drank and I ran.

One day out on a run, I discovered a historical plaque that I would never have seen from a car. It was titled "The Legend of the Turnips" and it explained how the Westport turnip, which it said was famous from Boston to Providence — not a great distance in our miles but huge apparently in the universe of turnips — was first grown in fields close by.

Who knew? This was almost as good as the monument to the chicken that stands in nearby Adamsville, R.I., another sight best viewed while pecking about in Reeboks.

Despite the heat, summer is the best season for running/jogging/walking/plodding. Get out there before winter comes and all the dogs turn into wolves and the show-offs in tiny shorts suffer frostbite in places that amuse the staff of emergency rooms.

Now the road beckons. Why, you could establish your own Legend of the Turnip — involving yourself as the little regarded plump vegetable who found new growth and became famous from here to down the street. Don't forget to say "good morning" to me as you plod by. Misery loves company. ✱

ON THE SHORES OF ERIE, LET THE DUCKPINS ROLL

Column, March 9, 2011

Mardi Gras can be celebrated in different ways. Would-be revelers can wear feathered costumes, drink lots of adult beverages, bare their breasts or — my own preference for inducing the bacchanalia mood — play in a duckpin bowling tournament. In Erie, Pa.

As it turns out (and who knew?), Erie is a hot nest of duckpin bowling. Once upon a time, when men were men and women were justly irritated, duckpin bowling was popular all over Western Pennsylvania and elsewhere.

For those too young to remember this bygone era, duckpin bowling is the close cousin of the better known 10-pin bowling. The dimensions of the lanes are the same but the duckpin balls are smaller and have no finger holes.

The pins so favored by ducks have rubber bands on them — gum bands, in Pittsburghese — and this is said to affect pin action. Not that I would know. My pins tend to remain inactive, despite my best efforts.

You may ask why duckpin bowling is called duckpin bowling. Do the participants waddle up to the lane and deliver the ball while making low quacking sounds? Only in my case. No, the reason is that before pin-setting machines, trained ducks would pick up the pins in their little beaks.

OK, I made that last bit up, because we duckpin bowlers like to amuse ourselves between frames. In fact, this is the one aspect of the sport I am good at. My experience has been

103

limited to a mixed league, which I was recruited to join about six years ago on the strength of my potato chip eating and beer drinking skills. Alas, these helpful talents did not make me a champion.

So I was honored to be asked to play at the interclub tournament in Erie this past weekend. Among certain duckpin bowlers, Erie is considered the holy of holies — well, not so holy considering the open bar, but certainly a mecca of duckpin pilgrims.

The interclub tournament was first held 61 years ago, and in the early years four clubs, three in the Pittsburgh area, would take turns hosting the tournament. But the years have put duckpin bowling to flight and now only Erie Maennerchor and the Edgeworth Club compete.

This year was Erie Maennerchor's turn to host, as it happens in the 140th anniversary year of its founding. I am told that *Maennerchor* translates from the German as "men's choir," and what a sadness it is that no ducks sang with them. The duckpin bowling takes place in the basement of an outwardly staid but inwardly magnificent building.

My bowling guru — who shall remain nameless, because you know the old saying: What happens in Erie, stays in Erie — had seen something in my bowling that others had missed: I was breathing and could fill out the roster. In gratitude, I agreed to share a room in a local hotel to defray expenses.

No doubt Erie has some fine hotels, but we didn't stay in one of those. We stayed in a hotel so run-down that it was beneath the dignity of bedbugs to live there, which I recognize isn't necessarily cause for complaint. However, this hotel had the tiniest towels I have ever seen. Apparently a group of poor jockeys were the hotel's last known guests.

I didn't care. I was ready to go. I had my bowling shoes. I had my monogrammed bowling shirt with my name unfortunately misspelled as *Res* instead of *Reg* — an error I was forced to accept because someone from a newspaper does not have much standing to complain about a typo on a shirt.

With advice from my guru/roommate to "just bowl your average," I proceeded to bowl under my average and the next day did worse than that. It was a performance so bad that everybody was moved to give friendly advice, such as "Have you thought of taking up cards?"

That night I slept fitfully in the fleabag hotel. Now even the fleas were giving me advice. The guru said I snored very loudly, but he did too. Between the two of us, we recreated the cannon fire of the Battle of Lake Erie in 1813, after which the American commander Oliver Hazard Perry famously wrote: "We have met the enemy, and they are ours. Have now gone duckpin bowling." (Careful readers will note some embroidery of the historical record.)

The next day I arrived at the club as a man inspired. I met the lanes and they were mine. All the good fellows cheered my hard-won battle for respectable mediocrity. In the spirit of Mardi Gras, I then had an adult beverage but I did not wear feathers or show body parts. It was the least I could do to repay Erie's abundant hospitality. ✤

WiTH ADViCE from my guru/ roommate to 'just bowl your average,' I proceeded to bowl under my average and the next day did worse than that. It was a performance so bad that everybody was moved to give friendly advice, such as 'Have you thought of taking up cards?

A FISH'S CAMP'S LURE LIES FAR FROM THE WATER

May 16, 2012

Before entering this column, readers should be alert to two advisories:

1) No fish were harmed in the production of this column.

2) Women readers should exercise discretion, because the subject matter concerns men behaving badly.

This is a tale about going back to an era when men were men and women, being women, laughed at them. Perhaps things haven't changed much.

You will understand this tale better if the words "fish camp" hold special meaning for you. For years now, those two words have tantalized my imagination.

In the beginning, a band of men left Pittsburgh and drove up to the northern woods of Pennsylvania for a few days of manly adventures. They did this every year, and I came to envy them.

And why would any man not envy them? Their activities were said to include eating (ravenously), drinking (excessively), laughing (outrageously), scratching (immodestly), boasting (prodigiously) and singing (off key-ly). Also, smoking cigars, telling dubious jokes, making impolite noises, ribbing fellow fish campers and shooting firearms ("Only when entirely sober, Your Honor").

Oh, and fishing. While the term fish camp may suggest fish putting up little tents on the bed of a river and singing campfire songs underwater, only men stay in fish camp. From time to time they put on waders and attempt to fly-fish for trout — "attempt" being the operative word because the trout remain pretty safe.

This year, I was invited to join the manly company of fish campers, standards not being what they once were. Was it my talent for dubious jokes that won the campers over? My ability to make impolite noises?

Whatever the reason, last weekend my dream came true and I became part of a long tradition. I went to a fish camp established in 1921 along Kettle Creek in Potter County.

They call this part of Pennsylvania "God's Country," and they are not far wrong. The Almighty did a wonderful job when he last vacationed here. It is a wild and beautiful place, and only a little more than a four-hour drive north and east from Pittsburgh.

There I fished amid the ghosts of scratching and laughing men of generations past, men who surely sang the fish camp song ("Men, men, men, men, men (low notes) ... Men! (high note) Wonderful men!").

Fish camp is just like you might imagine. It is in the middle of nowhere, far down a dirt road from civilization. Set in a valley amid wooded mountains, with a creek babbling nearby, fish camp is a modest bungalow big enough to hold six babbling men.

There is a small kitchen, a living room of sorts with a coyote skin hung over one beam to make the place feel homely, and a bunkhouse attached at the back.

Steaks were cooked on a small grill outside. Every few minutes someone would come by and put the lid up and someone else would then come by and demand the lid be down. In this way, the steaks were fanned to perfection by the lid going up and down.

WHILE THE TERM FISH CAMP

may suggest fish putting up little tents on the bed of a river and singing campfire songs underwater, only men stay in fish camp. From time to time they put on waders and attempt to fly-fish for trout – 'attempt' being the operative word because the trout remain pretty safe.

One of our campers was a notorious snorer — let us call him Joe — and he was required to sleep in the living room because it was feared that his snoring might attract bears looking for mates.

This seemed unfair. The bunkhouse sounded like the bears had already moved in and were cuddling my fellow campers, with the bunkhouse swaying on its foundations with every titanic snort. Meanwhile, in the next room, Joe quietly slept the sleep of the smugly innocent.

For those who cannot stand the din, an old-fashioned outhouse can be visited out back with old-fashioned reading material for those planning to sit a spell. You don't even have to bring your own spiders; they are supplied free. Fish campers think of everything.

Of course I had a wonderful time. It was a complete break, far from politics, far from the usual disputes, far even from cell phone communication. My only temptation was to pick up my dead cell phone and talk to myself about all the fish I didn't catch. Not a one.

I was dressed in all my fly-fishing gear — the rubber pants that gave me a frog-like air, the little jacket hung with flies and other equipment never needed — and yet the trout remained totally uncooperative. And was I sorry? No, because where else can a man stand up to his chest in water amid breathtaking scenery?

I have found a new hobby. And when I tire of eating, drinking and singing ("Men, men, men, men ... etc.") I am going to take up fly-fishing. I cast for trout, but I hooked contentment. ✳

Reg on patrol with Australian troops in Vietnam in 1970. When not doing Errol Flynn impersonations, his main job was to read the Aussie radio news on the American Forces Vietnam Network in Saigon.

Credit: John Fairley.

*Proud Dad Reg escorts daughter Allison on her
destination wedding day on a beach in Manuel
Antonio, Costa Rica, in 2009.*

*Katie Mendelson. son Jim, wife Priscilla and Reg. Jim and Katie were
married in October 2014.*

Allison and Critter Gilpin (who was born Christopher but was too energetic for his fomal name to stick) in Tahiti in 2014.

Jim and Katie on top of Gothics mountain in the Adirondacks in July 2014.

Credit: Sam Moody

Allison and Lucy in Tahiti.

Credit: © Stephen Govel

Reg and Tillie.

Priscilla and Tille, Reg and Lucy, Sewickley, Pa., in 2014.

Credit: Allison Gilpin.

CHAPTER FIVE

SCHOOL DAYS

AND DON'T DO ANYTHING I WOULD DO IF I WERE STILL YOUR AGE

Saturday Diary, Feb. 1, 1997

This is what I told my daughter, more or less:

Watch out for those Aussie boys — they are horrible rascals (your mother can confirm this). Beware of spiders and riptides. Be good.

Don't acquire an Australian accent - it's enough that I have one and it will only further confuse the dog. Don't lose your passport.

Do try the delicious meat pies. The beaches are great, but they can be treacherous, so only surf between the flags where the lifeguards are on duty (they're called life-savers down there). If they ring a bell, get out of the water immediately. That means a shark has been sighted.

Did I mention your passport and the spiders?

If you are caught in a rip, don't exhaust yourself but go with the flow. The current will eventually weaken and you will be able to get back to the beach, sharks allowing.

Take time to see the beautiful wild parrots. Listen to that ever jocular bird, the kookaburra, which just sits back and laughs at people from a great height – a role that in America is filled by members of Congress.

Remember, when you get to Sydney, you have Nothing to Declare. Be a good ambassador for your country and your school.

Nothwithstanding that beer is the national drink, don't have any. Try hard to remember that you are only 15. That also applies in regards to any horrible rascals that may look in your direction.

It is time to board. Of course, we love you and will kiss the dog on your behalf.

⌒

This happened a week ago at Pittsburgh International Airport and it was a hard thing to go through.

Allison, if she was nervous at all, was outwardly a picture of composure. We, her doting parents, were basically nervous wrecks.

She will spend five months at the Central Coast Grammar School, about 75 miles north of Sydney, in an official school-to-school exchange. She is staying with a lovely family whose own daughter stayed with us last year. And she was accompanied by a schoolmate, also on the exchange, on the 24-hour journey Down Under.

Everything about the adventure, then, should have inspired confidence. But as my wife so eloquently put it between sobs: ``My little baby is going to the other side of the world.'''

Fortunately, Allison's little brother was his usual unperturbed, down-to-earth self.

"Jimmy,'" I said, "as much as the thought will disgust and repel you, you need to hug and kiss your sister on this occasion."

"Certainly, Dad, I understand completely. And, for you, I can do it for only $3.'''

As parents of other 13-year-old boys will recognize, this constituted a real bargain.

And then she and her friend were going down the ramp. Waving frantically, blowing kisses, shouting garbled and frantic instructions ("`only kiss between the flags'''), we said our final goodbyes.

All through the rest of the day, all through the dark night and into the next long day, we willed our thoughts and prayers to lift the wings of distant planes.

Our anxiety was not helped by the fact that I have made this trip myself many times since I left Australia in 1973, and could imagine every step of the journey.

Our anxieties filled in the picture. Now is about the time she'll lose her passport. No, she's arrived, and she's already been attacked by spiders and sharks. No, get a grip - it's early yet, she's still two hours away from walking through the wrong aisle of the customs hall with the wrong luggage.

The vigil continued several hours after she was supposed to arrive — and still no word. We had to go out that evening, and we raced back to find a brief, reassuring message on the answering machine.

Phew! They had arrived safely, but the plane had been several hours late. As it turned out, it had to battle high winds across the Pacific and was forced to make an unscheduled landing in Fiji to refuel.

This is an extraordinary world we live in. It wasn't too long ago that parents took leave of their children and would hear nothing for months. They would post letters and summer would turn into winter before the mailman returned. ("Sorry, sir, this letter has come back for 2 cents postage!")

But among the many abominations of the modern world - talk radio, shopping malls and the general lack of shame - we at least have e-mail to bring the other side of the world closer.

Even the efforts of America Online, of which we are unhappy customers, cannot stop the communication.

It began almost immediately.

Activity news:

"We went for an hour-long bush — and I mean bush — walk and looked at the prettiest sights that overlooked a scene that looked a bit like Big Sur. Then we went swimming at a popular surfing beach with pretty big waves - don't worry, Dad, I stayed within the flags. Ha ha."

Descriptive news:

"I will try and explain about here for you. Tumbi Umbi is just a small place where people live - there is no town. There are so many more trees here than I expected and at night, when you go to bed, it sounds like you are in a jungle so I do not need to listen to my Jungle Magic tape - good thing because I forgot it."

Extremely reassuring news:

"This morning I went to my school and got my uniform. It is kinda ugly and the skirt is really long."

(That, a dad happily thinks, should keep the boys at bay for a while).

Nice words for little brothers:

"Jimmy, don't expect to keep the phone or Lava Lamp and do not take my money."

Answers to questions messaged from America:

"Koocaburos? (sic) Yes, I have heard them — they are very loud but I did not get a chance to see (one), or if I have, I didn't know that it was a koocaburo."

Between now and June, the e-mail lines are going to run hot between Tumbi Umbi, New South Wales, and Sewickley, Pennsylvania.

Little messages: Each serving as a charm to stave off a hundred fears, of rips and sharks and spiders and rascals. With luck, the edge of our anxiety will be dulled by descriptions of bush walks and laughing birds and all the blessings under the Southern Cross.

But nothing will completely fill the void until she is back safely. And who cares if she gets a new accent and confuses the dog? We will all be glad to see her. Why, even her little brother may give her a free hug. You never know. We live in an age of miracles. ✿

THE ROAD TO COLLEGE RUNS BACKWARD

Column, Aug. 4, 1998

All across America, they are on the road. With reference books, with concerned expressions, they make their pilgrimages.

They are parents and their senior high school children, and they are looking at colleges. Many, many colleges. At the end of these trips, they find that all the colleges have begun to blend into one great Generic University.

The students of the Class of '99, happily clueless to begin with, occasionally awaken from their teen torpor to pronounce favorably upon one college or another, using such well-known academic criteria as the tour guides being studly, cool-looking dudes or not.

Their parents, of course, would not know what is cool if they were standing on an iceberg. Parents, directed instinctually to be role models of squareness, are incapable of interpreting what young people like. All they know is that when they look at a likely college, they see a giant dollar sign with ivy on it.

So the whole enterprise is a sort of magical mystery tour for young people and their parents at a time when both parties would rather be at the beach. But at least everybody is together as a family, mostly cooped up in the car while traveling between schools and grouching at each other. In some optimistic circles, this is called quality time.

As it happens, the Henry family spent part of last week, interspersed between vacation, visiting several colleges in New England with their daughter.

Why not Pittsburgh, you say? Indeed, there are excellent schools in the Pittsburgh area, but our prospective college student feels that part of the experience is to get a million miles away from her parents and her younger brother, so she is currently considering schools with regard to their proximity to the Outer Solar System.

If I were your parent, you would understand this.

Well, as they say, there is a college out there for every student. All you have to do is find it amid the thicket of college recruitment mailings, the guide books, the fairs, the Web sites and videos and the erroneous information of fellow students.

In a simpler time, I imagine that a fond father would just call up his old alma mater and fix things up with the minimum of fuss: "I say, chaps, young Allison will be coming up next year. Just make sure she gets a good room on the quadrangle, will you?"

Actually, it is probably just as well that things are more democratic now. For example, I myself only graduated from the University of Hard Knocks, and when you go to an institution that just gives out degrees of concussion, you have nobody to call.

So instead we do the college tours. The admissions departments

IN MY EXPERIENCE, *the guide is crucial to a student's decision. The college you attend can mean what career you will follow, where you may live one day, perhaps even whom you will marry, and the whole train of events can depend on whether some college kid walking backward on a particular day shows nerdy tendencies.*

run these tours, usually with a student guide so as to give visitors an authentic flavor of the place.

These guides do an odd thing - they walk backward as they speak. This makes sense because they can then face the crowd as they give their commentary: "And on your left, we see the student lounge where we all goof off when we are supposed to be in class."

At this time, you can almost read the thought balloons rising above the crowd of visitors. All the high school seniors are thinking, "Phat!" All their parents are thinking, "Phooey!" On such impressions, students' lives turn.

It is actually quite frightening. In my experience, the guide is crucial to a student's decision. The college you attend can mean what career you will follow, where you may live one day, perhaps even whom you will marry, and the whole train of events can depend on whether some college kid walking backward on a particular day shows nerdy tendencies.

It occurs to me that the tour guides walk backward for another reason. A lot of thinking goes on at colleges, or so they say, so I suspect they are suggesting a metaphor for parents, preparing them for the day when their children themselves walk backward out of their lives, looking back all the while but striding ever farther into the future.

We will be sad on that day - not to mention broke - but for the moment, the search goes on. Education! It's a wonderful thing. ✱

AT LAST, THEY LEAVE HOME TOO SOON

Column, Sept. 7, 1999

No doubt it says something about my taste, but I have always thought that the saddest words in all literature are contained in the final chapter of "The House at Pooh Corner" by A.A. Milne:

"Christopher Robin was going away. Nobody knew why he was going; nobody knew where he was going .... But somehow or other everybody in the Forest felt that it was happening at last."

The transition from child to adult has many markers on the trail, but none so final and poignant as when a child leaves home for school.

Now, to be precise, I don't think Christopher Robin was going off to university when he left the Forest for the last time. He was probably headed for one of those notorious English boarding schools with the appalling food and poor central heating that build character.

So it is for the benefit of the Bureau of Strained Analogies that I stipulate that our Allison, who left for college this past weekend, is not Christopher Robin. Moreover, everybody knew why she was going and everybody knew where she was going.

They knew this because for weeks she and her friends have been consoling each other about the fact that their little group, which had gone through the thick and thin of high school life together, was now breaking up.

Because colleges do not all start together, they went off one by one, and each time there were farewells such as have not been seen since the parting of families beside the lifeboats on the Titanic.

The chorus wailed in a monsoon of tears: "It's Sarah's last night" — or, "Dear Briana's going tomorrow" — or, "Poor Deborah, we'll never see her again, well, at least until Thanksgiving."

Soon, tear ducts hung like saddle bags, and anxious parents feared that any more crying in the garden and the salt would kill the flowers and grass for at least the next generation.

Still, the parents would try to console their children without letting on that they thought that it was all rather ridiculous.

BECAUSE COLLEGES do not all start together, they went off one by one, and each time there were farewells such as have not been seen since the parting of families beside the lifeboats on the Titanic.

Finally, it was Allison's turn to go. She packed her stuff, then some more stuff, and then even more stuff for good measure. Explorers going on long safaris travel lighter than kids going to college. The trick is to pack every conceivable space without the family car actually starting to pop rivets. By the time she was done, there was hardly any space for her to sit.

After her brother gave her the traditional guy farewell - "See ya!" — she and my wife and I were off on the five-hour trip to upstate New York. We stayed in a motel and were at the college early next morning to sign in.

All the kids were milling about looking fresh-faced, and all the parents followed along suddenly feeling as old as the pharaohs. The registration process was very organized, and after about an hour of steady progress through the line, she had the key to her new life. Then began the process of putting the stuff in her room.

The room was only 15 feet by 10 feet, and with all her stuff, together with her roommate's bountiful stuff, the laws of physics and geometry would have to be suspended if they were to fit it all in. Other students had the same problem. Every few minutes another car, loaded to the bursting point, would pull up outside the dorm. Everywhere you looked, stuff.

Sad-faced dads would get the stuff and move the stuff inside. Then they would perform feats of ingenious carpentry to make shelves or rearrange beds. The mothers sorted and unpacked, becoming more morose by the minute.

In the meantime, the students were becoming happier and more relaxed, morning apprehension giving away to afternoon excitement. They had looked around the campus and noted that it was really an ivy-covered resort full of young people.

So they declared that their room, which had miraculously absorbed all their stuff, would be the official "cool room" of the dorm.

In the midst of their delight, the hour came at last for the parents to say goodbye to their little bear. The mother quickly put on her sunglasses, and the dad choked a little as he hugged her. And the happy daughter became the one to comfort her sad parents as they considered the stuff of life.

It comes full circle. They arrive as crying babies and we console them. They leave as smiling adults and they console us. ✤

A CELESTIAL SIGN OF CHANGING TIMES

Column, May 13, 2003

I am a great believer in omens. This does not mean that I worry about ladders or black cats, or consult the entrails of goats to look into the future (as it happens, the local Giant Eagle supermarket does not stock goat entrails, either fresh or frozen, although it is possible they lurk in the sausage section).

But it seems obvious to me that the Almighty sometimes gives us mortals a nudge and a wink by presenting certain situations so heavy in metaphorical implications that even the most shortsighted folk are likely to jump up and say: "Holy Toledo! It's an omen!"

Such was the situation in Geneva, N.Y., on Mother's Day, where family members were gathered in platoon strength for the graduation of Allison Henry at Hobart and William Smith Colleges.

Saturday was a nice day in the scenic Finger Lakes region, about a five-hour drive north and east of Pittsburgh, but on Sunday morning the great parade of storms that had caused devastation to western states and much excitement on the Weather Channel finally marched into Geneva.

School officials had switched the 10:30 a.m. commencement from outdoors to the field house, a smart move because it started to rain like the onset of a monsoon.

(A note of explanation about Allison's college: Certain schools around the country once consisted of a men's institution and a sister institution nearby. When the fresh winds of gender equality blew them together, the women's college, as in a traditional marriage, would give up its name.

Hobart College [the men's institution] and William Smith College [notwithstanding the male name, the women's] evolved differently. Today, for most practical purposes, they are the same. They have one president and take classes together.

Yet they retain separate residual identities, with separate deans, their own sporting monikers and colors, and they issue degrees in the name of each school at one commencement. Yes, it's a bit goofy; on the other hand, it seems to me it reflects perfectly the wished-for relationship of the sexes, equal but different.)

Now that I have explained that, let me just say that I am a great believer in bagpipes. As the young men and women of Hobart and William Smith filed into the spacious field house, they were led by the Mohawk Valley Frasers Pipe Band, who were in fine fettle.

There is nothing like the sound of bagpipes to stir the tearducts. It is not just that they sound like wailing cats — thus eliciting the natural sympathies of animal lovers. It is that they are pitched exactly to the emotional wells of our psychic being.

As a manly sort of fellow, I am not much for crying, reserving it for occasions such as being left with a large check in restaurants, but I fought back tears when I saw Allison come down the center aisle in her cap and gown, so confident and beautiful. On the swirl of pipes, parents all over the hall doubtless were being transported back to what seemed magically like yesterday — when their child came to college as a nervous freshman four years ago.

No sooner had the proceedings gotten under way than the heavens opened completely. The rain was falling on the field house roof now in a ferocious drum beat and great rumbles of thunder punctuated the speeches.

AS A MANLY SORT OF FELLOW, *I am not much for crying, reserving it for occasions such as being left with a large check in restaurants, but I fought back tears when I saw Allison come down the center aisle in her cap and gown, so confident and beautiful.*

As I thanked heaven for the good fortune that my daughter was graduating from an institution more prestigious than the University of Hard Knocks, as I did, I also praised Providence that I am not exalted enough to be at such a podium, battling not only a celestial percussion section but also the perception that I might be more full of wind than the Mohawk Valley Frasers Pipe Band.

More than two hours later, after the college president finally bid the new graduates a touching farewell, the doors were flung open. And, of course, the sun streamed in, the storm having passed, and everywhere relatives were saying: "It's an omen! It's an omen!" and, in that daylight of new optimism, there were hugs and picture taking of a Japanese-like intensity.

Then we went to back to Allison's little rented house, perhaps soon to be condemned by the local health department but more likely to be let to the next class of students. We raised a glass of champagne to Allison and her roommates, two Merediths and a Lauren. Good luck, girls, we said.

All across the country the same scene was surely unfolding — the parents feeling suddenly elderly and both glad and sad, knowing that another milestone had flashed by, and that the sun, though shining, was a little closer to setting. ✻

CMU DORM POLICY: NERDS GONE WILD?

Column, Feb. 28, 2007

Carnegie Mellon University, perhaps the finest academic institution in Pittsburgh and one of the best in the nation, has announced that it will allow opposite-sex students to share rooms under a pilot program in the fall.

Being a leading member of the fuddy-duddy community, I am against it, as this could start a new trend — already roughly 30 schools, private and public, are said to have some form of gender-neutral housing.

I find it shocking that these young people are allowed so much freedom in this modern era. Freedom is a precious right and should only be encouraged in countries which we invade and lay waste. At home, it merely causes people to become too free and easy.

My view is that people of all ages should behave and dress modestly, perhaps in head-to-toe garments impregnable to romantic overtures at all times. In the good old days, members of opposite sexes lived in separate digs patrolled by guard dogs and the cold showers ran non-stop.

Those were the days when a social stigma was attached to "living in sin." But young people are so bored and blase these days that they really do not know how to sin like we old-timers did. Why, they can't even be bothered to sneak around and commit sins. How can they feel any shame? They haven't worked hard enough to deserve it — haven't so much as distracted a guard dog.

But according to the Post-Gazette story by my friend Bill Schackner, himself very decorous, this housing program isn't about promoting sex (which would be unnecessary anyway given the fine job of promotion done by the mass media).

No, it is meant to enable students to choose the best roommate situation. Some are gay and perhaps don't want distractions. In other cases, the young men and women are just friends.

Well, I have mixed feelings about that. It seems to me that if you are going to live in sin, it shows great contempt for tradition not to actually sin if you have the opportunity.

And pity their poor parents who will worry because they assume their kids are doing "it," only to be concerned about whether they are normal when they learn the "it" the kids are doing is freshman calculus. (Not that there's anything wrong with doing calculus.)

That brings me to another concern. Carnegie Mellon University is a school for brainiacs, as evidenced by the fact that it is not easy to gain admission there. This year CMU had a record 22,052 applications for 1,360 freshmen places.

Of course, it would be hurtful and wrong to suggest that all Carnegie Mellon students are nerds. Still, if I were a young nerd about town instead of the handsome mature man of action that I am, I reckon I could do worse than be a CMU student.

As it happens, I saw lots of likely suspects for nerd-dom when I was up in Oakland last week, at least until I was escorted off campus for failing the random visitor IQ test.

Unfair or not, my fear is that nerdy kids at Carnegie Mellon might put aside writing computer language for the space program and attempt to brush up their knowledge of biology in the privacy of their own dormitories. This is wrong. Nerds should not be having love affairs with other nerds. There is always the danger that in the throes of nerd passion, their thick glasses will collide or else they will drop heavy laptops onto vulnerable body parts.

Quite part from that, it is nature's plan that smart people take partners who aren't quite as swift and need help with their gene pool so that the human race advances uniformly. That is what my wife did. Heck, that is what Laura Bush did.

... PITY THEIR POOR PARENTS

who will worry because they assume their kids are doing 'it,' only to be concerned about whether they are normal when they learn the 'it' the kids are doing is freshman calculus. (Not that there's anything wrong with doing calculus.)

Now don't go thinking that I am just down on young people, especially the few smart ones among them who attend Carnegie Mellon. Old coots long out of school should similarly keep to their own quarters unless they have formally taken the oath to love, honor, obey and accept all criticism.

Yet lots of old people do live together for reasons of convenience and not sin, fairly assuming that it is not a sin to use each other as human hot water bottles on the colder nights.

So perhaps we fuddy-duddies should just concede that in a free country in 2007, adults should be able to choose to live together for whatever reason. Perhaps we ought give the kids a break too, especially as those Carnegie Mellon kids aren't kids at all but adults, even if it drives us crazy that they are having so much fun. ✱

CHAPTER SIX

ALL iN THE FAMILY

A FATHER'S ODE TO THE JOY OF HIS LIFE

Column, March 27, 2001

It was 20 years ago today. No, Sgt. Pepper did not teach the band to play, but that day (night really) my heart and soul were full of music.

On March 27, 1981, my daughter Allison, our first child, was born in Magee-Womens Hospital. My wife and I had prepared for the big moment by equipping our little house with all manner of baby equipment, as well as by attending Lamaze classes and reading birthing books.

By the time Priscilla was ready to go into labor, we had studied so much that we felt like experts. We could find our focal point for purposes of birthing concentration and we could begin our breathing without a moment's hesitation. We were knowledgeable about counting the centimeters of dilation and could discuss the breaking of water at cocktail parties.

Indeed, if Priscilla had not been pregnant, I am sure we could have gone to the Third World with the Peace Corps and acted as para-obstetricians, shouting "begin your breathing" in exotic languages.

Such was the prelude of anticipation and excitement. So, of course, when the big moment finally came, about 5 a.m. on March 26, we didn't know what to do.

There is an old joke about a guy who wants to become a famous Shakespearean actor but the only part he can land is a walk-on role as a soldier. His one line is: "Hark, is that a cannon I hear?"

He's disappointed with such a modest part but resolves to make the best of it. So he practices every waking moment, often in front of a mirror. "Hark, is that a cannon I hear?" he says in a loud voice. "Hark, is that a cannon I hear?" he says in a low voice.

Finally, he is ready to wow the critics. The night of the performance comes, the curtain opens and the play proceeds. In the fourth act, he walks on stage holding his spear.

Then the cannon roars out his cue. Startled, he spins around and blurts out: "What the heck was that?"

That was sort of like it was for us — but the reverse. We were expecting the onset of labor to be a dramatic roar of a cannon, and what happened instead was anti-climactic. The labor pains were twinges, the other signs ambiguous. What the heck is this? Should we go to the hospital? We passed several hours in creative dithering. Finally, about 8 a.m., we called Magee and were advised to come in.

Thus began the long day's journey into night. The one smart thing I did was bring some bologna sandwiches, knowing that nothing fuels a supportive husband more than the timely ingestion of bologna. It was long and hard, and not just for Priscilla — I had long ago run out of sandwiches by the time Allison arrived about 1:30 the next morning.

I remember that the nurse put her on a table and I came forward and leaned over. She opened one little eye and closed it again. Presumably, she had seen enough.

She grew up, of course, as children have a habit of doing if you feed them. She grew into a charming little girl and then into a beautiful young woman, at all ages kind and good-hearted.

Birthdays are important milestones. (A digression to underline the point: My friend Dr. Jim Greenbaum from Kittanning turns 80 next Monday. As a pediatrician in Kittanning for years, Dr. Greenbaum looked after countless babies in the area. Congratulations, Jim.)

I write this column because Allison has been in South America since January, most of it in Ecuador, where she lived with a wonderful family in Quito. As a college sophomore, she is spending a semester studying Spanish and learning about the culture. She has far outstripped her father's knowledge of Spanish, which is limited to one useful phrase — *"cerveza, por favor."*

> # I REMEMBER
>
> *that the nurse put her on a table and I came forward and leaned over. She opened one little eye and closed it again. Presumably, she had seen enough.*

As she happens to be incommunicado at the moment, this is my birthday greeting to her.

Allison — March 27, 1981, was the happiest day of my life. It was happier than my wedding, for which I was tranquilized. It was happier than Jimmy's birth more than two years later (not because I didn't love the little fellow, but because by then this procreation stuff was old hat).

I left the delivery room walking on air and never really ceased. I, who once wondered whether I would ever get a date, had become a father. It was 20 years ago today. ✱

PHONE CALL FROM THAILAND LIFTS HEAVY BURDEN

Column, Jan. 4, 2005

This is how you know you are overweight: You go to Vietnam for Christmas and revelers in the street think you look like a beardless Santa Claus and one or two touch your stomach for luck in the manner of the lucky Buddha.

(Memo to self: Must lose weight in the New Year.)

Vietnam is not, I grant you, an obvious destination in the festive season, but the Henry family — father, mother, son — went there to see daughter Allison, 23, who has spent the past few months in Ho Chi Minh City teaching English and volunteering in an orphanage.

I blame myself for this odd turn of events. I first went to Vietnam 35 years ago as a soldier in the Australian army, and I fell in love with the country despite the tragedy of war. Four years ago I went back and found that peace had swept away the fear but not the beauty and the charm.

As a result of Allison picking up on my enthusiasm, the nightmare of every Pittsburgh parent became personal reality: Our baby moved away, and to old Saigon no less, a spot more outlandish than Cleveland.

At least in Cleveland you are safe from traffic on the sidewalks. That is not necessarily the case in Ho Chi Minh City. The traffic, 85 percent of it motorbikes, is truly crazy.

The most important piece of equipment of any Vietnamese vehicle is the horn, without which driving is impossible. Although everybody is honking at everybody else, and people are often driving on the wrong side of the road, running red lights and attempting insane maneuvers, no one blinks an eyelid and road rage is rare. Many thousands are killed on the roads every year in Vietnam, but the wonder is that every intersection isn't routinely the scene of mass carnage.

On Christmas Eve in Ho Chi Minh City, the normally nutty traffic was multiplied many times over as whole families piled on motorbikes to come downtown. The authorities had strung the main thoroughfares with lights, and a concert was staged in front of the Opera House.

Logically, Christmas shouldn't be a big deal in communist-ruled old Saigon, even with its small but significant Catholic presence. In fact, it was a huge deal. The people, with their cell phones and growing prosperity, were in the mood to be merry.

Perhaps much of it was simply Sparkle Season-Vietnamese style, and perhaps Santa says the only logical thing in the circumstances: "Ho, ho, Ho Chi Minh," but peace on Earth and good will among men were much in evidence.

It seemed like half the kids were dressed in Santa suits. When a grown-up Santa arrived in the lobby of our hotel, he was besieged by kids dressed as angels. And when one set of parents found that their child couldn't have a picture taken with Santa because of the crush, they did the next best thing: They found a pretty blonde American girl — that would be our Allison — sitting in the lobby and happily plopped the kid down on her lap for a photo.

When the public concert out in the street finished on the stroke of midnight with a sweet rendition of Silent Night, it seemed the best of Christmases and a Happy New Year seemed assured. What could possibly spoil it?

Yet unimagined by us and millions more, a great cataclysm was building in the bowels of the Earth under the Indian Ocean. By this time, our son Jim, 21, had left to make a side trip to Thailand to see his girlfriend from New York. He was to rejoin us in Hanoi in a few days.

He was in the pool at a resort on the island of Phuket when the first great wave struck. The water swept over the pool, but the two of them got out and managed to have the presence of mind to get to higher ground before two bigger waves arrived with deadlier force. If they had been in their room, they would have died.

As it was, the resort was destroyed and they lost everything except their lives and their bathing suits — no passports, no money, no proper clothes. I had our first inkling of trouble when I saw a brief bulletin on a TV set at the airport as we prepared to board our flight to Hanoi.

When Jimmy did not arrive on his flight, and the hours wore on and we heard nothing from him, fears that seemed surreal began to seem more and more plausible. A couple of times that terrible night I walked the streets of Hanoi alone

WHEN THE PUBLIC CONCERT

out in the street finished on the stroke of midnight with a sweet rendition of Silent Night, it seemed the best of Christmases and a Happy New Year seemed assured. What could possibly spoil it?

139

and in despair just to get away from the TV and the pictures of carnage from Phuket and elsewhere. The grim absurdity of it was striking: We had always worried about Allison in Saigon and here was Jimmy perhaps lost to a tsunami in Thailand.

Then he called — on a borrowed cell phone — and we all cried in our joy and relief to hear that they were safe and unharmed. They would soon return home, their only lasting scars the contemplation of those few minutes when paradise turned into hell.

Now that the dread has lifted from me, although not the sorrow for others, I feel I should rub my own stomach. Surely no Buddha was ever so lucky. ✱

YES, YOUNG MAN, YOU MAY TAKE HER HAND

Column, Oct. 1, 2008

We interrupt this global financial crisis for a news bulletin that is more important, at least to me: My daughter is getting married.

Longtime readers of my work — and let me just say that counseling is available — will recall me writing about Allison Henry over the years:

How when she was born she opened one little eye and saw me for the first time, then closed it, thinking perhaps there had been some mistake.

How I used to go crazy at her lacrosse and field hockey games in high school, often shouting at the referees because their whistle blowing was interfering with her goal scoring, which seemed a reasonable objection at the time.

How she went away to school in Australia for six months in her sophomore year with the warning not to develop an Aussie accent in case our Sandy the Wonder Dog became further confused.

How she finally graduated from high school and went off to college amid scenes of tearful teen anguish not seen since friends said goodbye on the boat deck of the Titanic.

How she played rugby in college against a visiting team comprising such terrifying women that I thought perhaps I had dated some of their mothers.

How she graduated from college with bagpipes wailing, not to mention parents wailing.

How she got her first job as a kindergarten assistant back in the Pittsburgh area and I came to her class to read a Curious George book with my favorite character in all literature, The Man in the Yellow Hat.

How she went off to Vietnam for six months to teach English as a foreign language and her mother, brother and I came to visit. That was the time Vietnamese children rubbed my stomach for luck — which turned out to be needed because]her brother, Jimmy, took a side trip to the island of Phuket in Thailand and the first wave of the tsunami broke over his head as he swam in a resort pool. Fortunately, he reached a place of safety and was able to continue the work of being a lifelong irritation to his sister.

How she moved to New York City and became a first-grade (and now second-grade) teacher in a boys' private school. How she came back to Pittsburgh for a visit, after Sandy the Wonder Dog had gone to the great couch in the sky, and declared that "this family needs a dog," quickly found Sooner the Needy Dog and then just as quickly went back to New York leaving her parents to cope with the new dog's many needs.

After all these adventures, Allison has announced her engagement to Christopher Gilpin, also a teacher, who grew up in the Boston area and has been known since childhood as Critter. Ideally, a father does not look for a prospective son-in-law named for a small furry animal but, to look on the bright side, it's better than "Monster." For my part, I am just glad they are getting married.

Critter, whom I sometimes call Cricket by mistake, is a good guy and he did the proper thing by calling us up from New York and asking for our daughter's hand in marriage. As she is 27 years old, this was not strictly necessary.

Unfortunately, I was mowing the lawn at the time and after Critter asked for permission to marry Allison — in truth somewhat jokingly, aware that he was giving a modern ironic nod to traditional practice — I gave them my blessing and we chatted briefly.

Why not? We are two guys and guys don't have to string out a two-minute conversation into half an hour of ooh-ing and aah-ing in a great show of emotion and sensitivity over possible flower arrangements and bridesmaids' dresses.

So, after the minimal manly pleasantries, I got to the point: "This is great news, Critter, but I have to go now — I have to finish mowing the grass before it gets dark." Of course, being a good guy, he understood entirely.

Allison's mother, however, not being a guy and not being fluent in guy-speak, was not amused to hear this. "How could your future son-in-law call you up to say he and Allison were getting married and you cut him short to cut the yard?!" I fear I have not heard the last of it.

So I am thinking that at the reception we could have little lawn mowers on the tables as party favors. As Allison is not getting married until next September, we have quite a few mowings to think about it. Oh, that will be a happy day if I don't say something more stupid. ✽

SO, AFTER THE MINIMAL MANLY PLEASANTRIES,

I got to the point: "This is great news, Critter, but I have to go now — I have to finish mowing the grass before it gets dark.

POCKETS EMPTIED, A PROUD FATHER LETS GO

Column, April 1, 2009

Once upon a time the only destination for a father of the bride was the poorhouse, but the trend of destination weddings has changed all that. The poorhouse now comes after a visit to an exotic locale.

This explains what I was doing on a recent Saturday on a beach in Manuel Antonio, Costa Rica, dressed in coat and tie and loafers with little tassels on them, which is not what I usually wear to the beach.

My daughter, Allison, was wearing her wedding dress.

It was late afternoon. The sun was low in the tropic sky and the coconut palms were waving at the sea. The guests were seated facing the surf on little pews that had been rented, I suppose, from the Costa Rican equivalent of Pews R Us.

The guests had faced a challenge coming this far. They found themselves in a paradise of bountiful creation.

Monkeys were everywhere in this Garden of Eden and I am glad to report they knew better than to mess with the sort of person who would wear tasseled loafers to the beach.

I was particularly impressed with the howler monkeys. How they howl! Their calls are a great Jurassic Park-like roar. I can only surmise that the males were trying to get in the last word with their spouses. Poor underevolved creatures. I did not have the heart to tell them that this was impossible.

We saw sloths. I had never seen a sloth before, at least outside a government agency. Birds were abundant, too, and one morning a pair of toucans perched in the tree outside our room. As I remarked at the time, two can but three's a crowd.

In the days before the wedding, we went zip lining, which is what all potentially suicidal tourists do. The idea is that you are attached by hooks to a wire so that you can zip above the canopy of the rainforest and take in the sights.

Forget the sights. Traveling at the speed of light, you spend all your time suppressing a shriek while figuring out how you can avoid hitting the tree at the other end. One of our party did hit a tree and it was very painful for him. The laughter of his friends afterwards was especially bruising.

While I did not hit any trees, I was mortified to be chosen for a special industrial-strength harness that I believe the guides use for the larger adventurers they fear may come untethered and leave craters on the forest floor.

When it came time for the guests to gather on the beach for the ceremony, they were tired, happy, sprained, bruised and burned to a crisp.

In that latitude close to the equator, the sun shines fiercely and some people got burned through their shirts or under beach umbrellas. Fortunately, I had time to get know these guests before they became human lobsters.

Such was the prelude to the hour I had been waiting for all my adult life. Allison stood at my side, looking radiant and beautiful in the traditional way of brides.

True, I had not imagined it like this. We waited in the shadows of tropical foliage for Gen. Rommel in high heels — that would be the coolly efficient wedding planner — to give the command to advance.

To my right, at the end of the public beach, locals were playing soccer. To my left, I saw the human lobster guests sitting on the open-air pews, holding their programs in their claws and wondering if they might self-combust in the setting sun.

Then the violinist struck up the march as the booming surf provided the percussion section. A father's pride kept me sublimely calm. I registered little beyond joy as we walked up the coconut-studded path.

I did notice that just about everybody else was dressed with sensible casualness, including the bridegroom, in contrast to me, the father of the bride, whose solemn duty was to assume a look that would deter monkeys.

SUCH WAS THE PRELUDE

to the hour I had been waiting for all my adult life. Allison stood at my side, looking radiant and beautiful in the traditional way of brides.

This done, I muffed the only line I had, then delivered Allison to her new husband, Christopher Gilpin, aka Critter, and took my place off to the side.

At one point during the ceremony, I remember seeing a fat fellow in a bathing suit jogging slowly along the beach behind the happy couple. I felt like yelling to him, "Hey, buddy, I am the only big-harness-size guy allowed on this beach. Why don't you zip off?" But I forever held my peace, because I knew we could Photoshop him out of the wedding pictures later.

This is how we lost a daughter but gained a Critter. That night I danced with Allison to a Beatles song ... "In my life / I love you more." Ah, bring on the poorhouse. I am rich in memories. ✿

A NEW BABY'S ABOUT AS GRAND AS IT GETS

Oct. 5, 2011

As we grow older, the hardest of the youthful attributes to retain is cuteness.

Some elderly people do manage the trick of being cute, but usually it involves aids such as shawls and rocking chairs, not the natural glow of all-weather cuteness that is the special blessing of the young.

Unfortunately, some of us were a little short-changed in the cute department from the beginning. My moment of being cute came one Monday morning in 1954 — or was it that Tuesday in 1953? In any event, what a shock it was to my mother.

That is why I have always strived for something else — a lively sense of humor, a pleasing personality, an inquiring mind, all of which obviously are still a work in progress.

But as the years have begun to flash by like mile markers passed in a speeding antique sports car, my hopes have turned to some other attribute more suitable for the autumn of my life.

It occurs to me that I have always lacked grandeur, and that would be something to work on. Wouldn't it be grand to be grand? Lo and behold, I can report today that I have achieved this unlikely status.

On Sept. 28, I became a grandfather for the first time, thanks to my daughter Allison. She gave birth to a 7-pound, 6-ounce daughter at the Royal Hospital for Women in Sydney.

Matilda Grace Gilpin will be known as Tillie so those Aussie boys won't think they can just go Waltzing Matilda with her.

With apologies to James Brown, I will pause now for a revised rendition of the famous song:

I feel good, I knew that I would, now
I feel grand, just as I planned, now
So good, so grand, I got you

My daughter has apparently decided to live my life in reverse. As you know, I left Australia and, after many adventures, settled in Pittsburgh.

Allison was born in Pittsburgh and, after many adventures, moved to Sydney last year with her husband from the Boston area, who is known as Critter (good thing too, because he has become a surfer dude, and Christopher, his given name, is too formal for the beach).

Thirty years ago, I called Australia from a pay phone at Magee-Womens Hospital in Pittsburgh at about 2 in the morning to tell my parents in Australia that Allison had been born and she was very cute and they, grandparents already, were really grand now.

Likewise, about 2 a.m. Pittsburgh time on Sept. 28, although it was about 4 in the afternoon in Sydney, Critter called on a cell phone from the Royal Women's Hospital to say that Tillie was born and she was a princess of cuteness — which was perhaps to be expected, coming from a royal hospital — and we, Allison's parents, were now as grand as grand could be.

On the home front, the hours preceding this fateful announcement were their own sort of heavy labor. Thirty years ago, the stork's progress was not charted by cell phones and text messages, even video on Skype — just a simple call after the stork had landed with the baby. Mother and daughter are fine, call you tomorrow; that was about the extent of the information.

But for a day and a half before Tillie arrived, the calls and text messages bounced between Australia and America marking every part of the journey — timing of contractions, centimeters of dilation, morale of mother, etc.

As the night wore on, the break between calls and texting grew longer — which was taken at Baby HQ as a Very Bad Sign. But finally, Critter, after a long and ominous silence, sent a text: "Call immediately."

And the grandmother-to-be did call and couldn't get through, and urgent text messages were sent saying we couldn't get through, and there was wailing and unseemly oaths and rending of night garments. Just then Critter sent a photo of a baby taken on his cell phone — a cute baby — but what variety of baby? Boy or girl? Allison and Critter had decided against finding out the gender in advance.

And just when frustration and excitement were just too much for potentially grand people to bear, Critter called to announce that the picture was of Matilda "Tillie" Grace.

And in that moment of high elation, I thought I heard the beat of angel's wings carrying across the vast

> **BUT FOR A DAY AND A HALF** before Tillie arrived, the calls and text messages bounced between Australia and America marking every part of the journey — timing of contractions, centimeters of dilation, morale of mother, etc.

ocean, but in truth it could just as well have been the stork flying off and grumbling: "I'm outta here. It's not like the old days."

Ah, but these are grand days, too. ✿

IN-LAW WAS EXTRAORDINARILY GREAT SURPRISE

Column, Dec. 28, 2011

When a new year huddles in the wings, waiting to be introduced with popping champagne corks and the strains of "Auld Lang Syne," opinion writers are instinctively driven to make lists — lists of the best and worst of the old year, lists of predictions for the new.

Today I give you a best list with just one name, that of the most remarkable person I ever met in my life.

To see him around Orange Park, Fla., where he had his last home, you would not have thought so. He was tall and distinguished, certainly, and when he spoke it was with an exaggerated English accent delivered in booming tones often punctuated by laughter.

But to look at him you might think his tailor was the local thrift shop — and you might have been right. The charming old guy everybody knew as Barny was not one for formalities in dress or manner.

I first met Barny some 35 years ago in London, where he was born and where I was then working. He was married to the mother of my American girlfriend. Barny was her stepfather.

If she was ever going to be more than my girlfriend, the first hurdle we had to pass was to meet the parents, as terrifying a ritual as any in nature.

To further complicate my chances of future happiness, I was an Aussie newspaperman, which put me in the British social ranks somewhere between bricklayer and bus conductor.

Social graces? I had only heard of them. My talents were not then obvious (hold your wise remarks), my prospects dim.

To put me at my ease my girlfriend told me about her mother, herself a gracious lady, and stepfather. ("Oh, by the way, his full name is the Honorable Barnaby J. Howard and he is the second son of Lord Strathcona and Mount Royal. He spent his summers growing up on the Scottish island of Colonsay in the Inner Hebrides.")

HE WAS TALL AND DISTINGUISHED,

certainly, and when he spoke it was with an exaggerated English accent delivered in booming tones often punctuated by laughter. But to look at him you might think his tailor was the local thrift shop — and you might have been right.

So I went shaking in my plebeian boots to meet her parents, knowing that I was about to bomb in a way that would recall the London Blitz.

And when I met the Honorable, he was as warm and friendly as could be. "Come in old boy, I'm Barny. What would you like to drink?" (This quote is a reconstructed best guess, because at the time I was too petrified to think.)

Against all odds, I did not break any crockery. I did not burp. I did not say the wrong thing. All the stereotypes I held about how superior, upper-class Englishmen were supposed to behave immediately shattered. A year or so later, my girlfriend became my wife, led down the aisle by Barny in the absence of her deceased father.

Barny, when he was not greeting dubious suitors, was a storyteller like no other. The best story was his life.

It was an adventure in four parts. First, he attended Eton College, where the boys wear top hats and tails but do not become magicians when they grow up — just important English persons. The Second World War was on and Barny had to patrol the campus at night as a warden looking for incendiary devices.

Upon graduation, he joined the Royal Navy to be a flier, but he was sent to the United States to train. He finally received his wings in Corpus Christi, Texas, and was offered the chance to join an operational U.S. Naval Reserve unit flying F4U Corsairs out of the naval air station at Jacksonville. The war soon ended but his happy memories of Jacksonville never did. His last home was in sight of the airfield.

After the war he attended Trinity College, Cambridge, and then went to Africa to make his own fortune. He spent about 20 years in Southern Rhodesia, now Zimbabwe, where he made a farm out of rough bush — a place of baboons and leopards and characters even more eccentric than Barny.

In middle age, he attended a life-changing course at Harvard Business School, married my wife's mother, came back to live permanently and happily in the United States and set up a successful investment company specializing in small businesses.

A week before Christmas, Barnaby J. Howard — flier, farmer, investor, husband, father, cheerful companion — died at home at age 86, to be mourned by his last wife, Evie, and friends and family on at least three continents.

At New Year's, should auld acquaintance be forgot? Never! For here was the most remarkable man, a born aristocrat but more importantly a man of natural nobility, and in my sorrow I just had to remark. �֍

BEST CHRISTMAS GIFT EVER CAME TO THE DOOR

Dec. 26, 2012

'Twas a night before Christmas, when all thro' the house, not a creature was stirring, not even a mouse.

Then the phone rang.

It was our friend Lisa, whose tall and slender frame is animated by abundant energy and extravagant personality. "Are you in bed?" she asked the sleepy Mama of the house.

"Yes." (Of course, yes — it was about midnight and not a creature was stirring, not even a husband.)

"Well, I am coming over in five minutes," Lisa said. "You have to see the most exciting thing ever!"

Five minutes passed, punctuated by a drowsy thought: What could be more exciting than sleep on a weeknight?

The doorbell rang. The Mama of the house put on her dressing gown and went downstairs. I remained in bed, because it is not my habit to receive women with large personalities after business hours.

Suddenly, shrieks, crying and more shrieks erupted. Then a bellowed order: "Reg, come down here quick!" That got my attention. I quickly threw on a pair of sweatpants, not knowing whether I might have to punch Santa Claus in the nose or give him milk and cookies.

But what to my wondering eyes should appear, but ... my daughter Allison.

Wait! That couldn't be true. Allison lives in Sydney, Australia, with her husband and their daughter (our grandchild)

Matilda, known as Tillie. It's at least a 20-hour trip on a couple of flights to Pittsburgh. We thought they were going to have Christmas in Australia, where Santa uses kangaroos rather than reindeer because they can carry extra presents in their pouches.

Then I saw Tillie; her cheeks were like roses, her nose like a cherry and she would be a right jolly elf if only she weren't screaming from all the grandmotherly shrieks that marked her entrance.

But what about Lisa? She was a co-conspirator to keep the visit secret and in the middle of the night drove them home from the airport.

Surprise, surprise! Of course, we were not surprised, just utterly shocked. It wasn't until I kissed Allison and felt a real cheek that I was sure I wasn't dreaming. But even now it seems like a dream.

At 15 months, Tillie is toddling now, making trips around the house in search of biped adventure. She points at some things and makes little chuckles at others, all the while delivering a commentary in a language known only to other babies.

The only sadness is that Allison's husband could not make the trip from Sydney because he works in retail and the shopping must proceed regardless of geography. Critter, as he is universally known, is a good father. If he were here, it would not be accurate to say that all thro' the house not a creature was stirring, because Critter is in perpetual motion, often entertaining his daughter.

As the grandfatherly duty officer for this trip, I am trying to fill the vacuum as best I can. One of my favorite tasks is to read to Tillie. She is particularly fond of a book called "Snuggle Puppy," a work with which I was not previously acquainted. It takes the form of a love poem or song and, as I read it, I think I am the old dog and Tillie is the snuggle puppy.

Ah, there's nothing like a real book. When Tillie grows up, or even when she grows from tiny to small over the next few months, she may be beckoned by Pied Piper technology and find her books on an iPad or Kindle. E-books are all well and good, but can they survive an attack of Rice Krispies and scrunched banana that babies use to express their appreciation? I think not.

AT 15 MONTHS,

Tillie is toddling now, making trips around the house in search of biped adventure. She points at some things and makes little chuckles at others, all the while delivering a commentary in a language known only to other babies.

I have another reservation about electronic books. It is hard to write a dedication on them. The other day, I was going through our bookcase, so ordered by a higher authority to thin the ranks of books — my paper friends — in the interest of eliminating the dreaded domestic clutter.

There I came across "The Coral Island" by R.M. Ballantyne, the first non-picture book I ever owned, given to me by my parents. It was a tip-top boy's yarn about pirates (allow me here a sentimental "Arrgh"). On the first blank page, my mother had written in her frail hand "Happy Christmas Reggie from Mother & Dad, Christmas '56."

Before she leaves, I want to give Tillie a signed, old-fashioned book. "Thank you and your Mom for making this our best Christmas ever, the most exciting thing ever, your old dog Papa, Christmas 2012."

Happy Christmas to all, and to all a good night. ✳

THERE'S ONE MORE CUTE LITTLE AUSSIE TO VISIT

Column, April 2, 2014

When you are apart from the people and things you love, life often unfolds as a series of snapshots, not as a continuous rolling film.

For grandparents in particular, the lights-camera-action moments can only be experienced by traveling long distances. And that explains why I am just back from Australia, where I grew up and where my daughter Allison, who was born in Pittsburgh, is living my life in reverse. Except the part about writing a newspaper column. She is way too smart for that.

Allison has settled in Sydney with her husband Christopher, who is originally from Boston and is known to everyone as Critter, although he is not really a critter, just unusually quick and feral in his movements. He could do wallaby impersonations if he weren't always leaping about on a surfboard.

Allison and Critter Gilpin are the proud parents of a new baby, Lucy Louise, now 4 weeks old, who joins her little big sister Tillie, now 2 1/2 years old.

Once Lucy was born, the international cute signal went off — "Cute, cute, cute, calling all grandparents, cute, cute, cute." So we lost no time, traveling 24 hours in the economy cattle class of airplanes from Pittsburgh, to see the new baby, the mother and the surfing wallaby.

And, imagine our surprise, little Lucy was as cute as advertised, although — as I often say — it's easy being cute if you are a baby. It's being cute at 66 years old and above that is the challenge. Of course, I am not in the least biased, but Lucy is fluffy cloud cute. Indeed, as I cradled the wee child, an old Beatles song kept playing in my mind, only with a Down Under twist to the lyrics: "Lucy in the sky with Vegemite."

(International-minded readers will recognize that Vegemite is the edible axle grease that Aussies put on their toast to make themselves tough.)

IMAGINE OUR SURPRISE,

little Lucy was as cute as advertised, although — as I often say — it's easy being cute if you are a baby. It's being cute at 66 years old and above that is the challenge.

Tillie is good with her new sister, bending down to give her a kiss at every opportunity. Indeed, Papa — that would be me — was jealous of this because Tillie, herself a blond, blue-eyed pixie, has become more discriminating about kissing visitors from America, even if closely related. Her mother has taken to calling her Little Miss Attitude. It is further proof that the Terrible Twos are a worldwide phenomenon.

I understand her reservations. If I were small and cute in my own right, I too would object to large, wrinkled persons who have failed the cuteness test wanting to hug me. Allison says this is just a phase. Of course it is. But I'd jump off the Sydney Harbor Bridge if it didn't cost about $250 to climb it.

Still, we had fun. We took Tillie to the famous Taronga Park Zoo, where we saw a platypus, a wombat, a tree-climbing kangaroo, lions, tigers and, oh my, a huge silver-backed gorilla, which Tillie did not like — perhaps thinking he looked a bit like Papa, although perhaps I am being a little sensitive. After all, the gorilla had more hair.

We went to the library with Tillie, who loves books. She picks up books and has a great time pretending to read them in a little Aussie accent as Lucy sits nearby and squeaks in a tiny Aussie accent.

We went to Tillie's ballet class. Dancing has not been a traditional strength of our family — occasionally someone's pants will catch fire and he or she will bust a few moves — and it will take dancing lessons at 21/2 to break the trend.

Or not. Tillie certainly wears a fine tutu. Her dancing consists of running across the studio, with a wallaby prance she gets from her father, while imitating a blossom. She did this until one of her little pals did an errant pirouette and sent her sprawling. Then she spent the rest of the class on injured reserve.

This was the story of the people we loved as the action unfolded, quite different from the snapshot impressions gained intermittently on Skype — closer, more complicated.

Unfortunately, Sydney with its glorious beaches and harbor is one of the world's most expensive cities. If you get off the plane and experience a throbbing in your side, it may not be deep vein thrombosis. In Sydney, it may turn out to be deep wallet thrombosis.

All I can say is that it is worth the pain, especially if you are surrounded by dolls of various sizes. All grandparents know that feeling, wherever they are. ✳

CHAPTER SEVEN

POLITICS, THE DESPAIR OF ALL

ELECTION DAY POTBOILER PRESENTS A NOVEL IDEA

Column, Nov. 21, 2000

A hastily written book follows every headline-generating event in America. But, so far, no one has come out with a potboiler on Election Debacle 2000.

At least not until now. Fortunately, I have dashed one off by toiling night and day out of a sense of deep civic responsibility — that, and the chance to make a quick buck.

Of course, some liberties have been taken. For example, I have inserted myself into the action as a hard-bitten, sentimental, debonair Florida columnist. Only modesty prevents me from suggesting that Burt Reynolds would be good for the part in the much-anticipated movie version.

The following excerpts are for your holiday reading pleasure. I call my little novel:

DAY OF INDECISION

Chapter 1

The palm trees rustled in the gentle sea breeze and the hot Florida sun streamed through the apartment window, reflecting sunlight off the sleeping bald head of Rege Hialeah. A beam fell upon the curtains, which soon erupted into flame.

"What the heck!" exclaimed the hard-bitten columnist, smoke filling his finely flared nostrils as he leaped from bed in one debonair motion. He quickly doused the fire with the contents of a spare beer bottle.

He was shedding a sentimental tear for the drapes when the phone rang. It was the editor they called Vulture.

"Hialeah, if you want to get material for your column, I suggest you get your lazy butt down to a polling station in West Palm. Strange things are happening."

"But tomorrow's column was going to answer the most burning question of the day," Hialeah pointed out.

"You mean, 'Who let the dogs out?' " Vulture said.

Chapter 2

Concerned senior citizen Edna Addled was up early and rarin' to go. The palm trees had barely started rustling in the gentle morning breeze when she arrived at the First Community

Church of the Heavenly Mall. She had waited a long time for this moment.

"Is this where the bingo is?" she asked the nice young people handing out leaflets.

Samantha Portfolio, wearing a "Dubya for Big Enchilada" sash over her opulent bosom, shook her large blond hairdo and smiled at Edna. "Why, surely ma'am. You just remember to punch your card with as many holes as you can."

Chapter 3

(The obligatory sex scene)

Samantha's cotton dress clung hard to her lithesome body in the lush heat, which had been getting hotter by the second since she had sighted Rege Hialeah stepping out from behind a palm tree.

Hialeah strolled over with a debonair air. "Hi, babe," he whispered seductively. "Any chance I could dimple your chad?"

"I wouldn't want my chad to become pregnant," she said coyly.

"No chance of that if we practice 'safe' tallying — just keep your white gloves on," he advised.

Then he winked a sentimental wink. "I promise I won't leave your chad hanging," he said.

The charming, silver-tongued rascal! She took him by the hand and led him into a booth.

Chapter 10

Dan Rather had declared the state of Florida for the Democrats, or at least so it seemed. As a precaution, his remarks had been sent to the Institute of Mysterious Metaphors in Tallahassee for further analysis.

Feisty senior Edna Addled was pleased and elated while at the same time angry and confused. She was like a palm tree bending this way and that in the not-so-gentle breeze.

"Who is this Pat Buchanan I seemed to have punched my card for? I hope he is a nice young man."

DAN RATHER had declared the state of Florida for the Democrats, or at least so it seemed. As a precaution, his remarks had been sent to the Institute of Mysterious Metaphors in Tallahassee for further analysis.

Chapter 17

The palm trees were all but obscured by lawyers. Everywhere you looked, lawyers. They were thicker than alligators on the community golf course, but, of course, they were not as trustworthy.

A gale of legal claims and counterclaims whipped up the sand. Ordinary citizens, innocently driving their golf buggies and bicycles, had to stop every few moments to free wheels clogged with flying writs.

Chapter 23

"Darndest bingo I was ever at," Edna Addled exclaimed.

SEVEN DEADLY SINS ARE ON THE MARCH

Column, Feb. 1, 2005

When President Bush delivers his State of the Union speech this week, he will describe America firmly in step on the march of freedom while ascending to the sunlit slopes of prosperity situated at the very foot of heaven.

As he speaks under the great dome, the esteemed members of Congress, their cheeks flushed with excitement, will sing hosannas to the president like so many cherubim around the golden throne, excepting, of course, certain Democrats, who will sit on their hands and make faces as if suffering from gastric distress.

All this you know. What you don't know is that in another place, where the central heating is very hot, the Prince of Darkness (no, not Bill O'Reilly) will deliver an alternative address to the citizens of that grim abode. This will be his annual State of Disunion address, relating how America fared in the Seven Deadly Sins department in 2004.

You may wonder how I got an advance copy of this speech, which is usually damnably hard to find.

Well, in 38 years in journalism, I have met many rogues who have since become handy contacts in the nether regions.

These lost souls were not just politicians, but also people from my own impious business, and they inhabit all parts of hell, including the very last circle, which is reserved for copy editors doomed eternally to put commas into sentences and take them out.

Here is an abridged version of the speech to be delivered by Evil Inc.'s CEO, and please spare me any observation about the devil being in the details:

My fellow evil doers,

It is my low honor and privilege to be speaking to you tonight and to report that the Seven Deadly Sins are deadlier than ever, and, as a result, disunity is flourishing like never before.

(Pause here for the clapping of cloven hooves and the banging of pitchforks).

Some of you may doubt my words in light of the current president of the United States using his office as a bully pulpit for his moral values and dedicating his every waking moment to committing faith-based initiatives. And I'll be the first to admit that this has led to much gnashing of teeth in the demon community.

But, as we say down here, the tar pot is always blackest before it comes to the boil. We have long sponsored a program to send false prophets into the midst of the American people to aim bile at convenient scapegoats — liberals, gays, you name it — while ostensibly preaching a gospel of love. It has worked a charm. These accomplished villains actively embrace politics, an enterprise so unholy as to make the likes of us shrink away in horror.

To be sure, many saintly priests, pastors and lay people remain to vex us with their wretched insistence on practicing what they preach (shudder), but thankfully religion for many Americans has become an excuse to be judgmental and sanctimonious at the expense of others.

As they might say in Texas, these pious buckaroos are all bishop's hat and no compassionate cattle.

In this hypocritical environment, the Seven Deadly Sins have recorded outstanding growth. Take pride, for example, one of our ancient favorites.

I do not have to tell you how much it cheers my cold heart to see America's rulers so puffed up with pride that they can barely admit — or even think of — a single mistake they have made. Even now, their arrogance is spurring them to undermine the Social Security system, which will be a great thing for us down here, of course, in that it will be break the faith of the elderly on that happy day when they are destitute and forced to take in laundry.

As for envy, the whole country is envious of celebrities, whom Americans have set up as their new gods. Of course, envy goes hand in hand with greed, a sin for which we can thank the corporate community for having set such sorry standards. Fortunately for us, Americans are too slothful to demand a change.

And let's hear it for gluttony! Need I say more? By the way, diabolically delicious doughnuts are available in the back of the hall for those feeling peckish. Some are a bit toasted.

As for anger, just turn on any talk radio station. Whoa! They are going to be talkative and angry when they finally get down here.

My only regret is in the area of lust. Unlike his predecessor, the current occupant of the White House is

AS FOR ENVY, the whole country is envious of celebrities, whom Americans have set up as their new gods. Of course, envy goes hand in hand with greed, a sin for which we can thank the corporate community for having set such sorry standards. ...

not setting the wrong example. Americans seem to be sinning quite well without his guidance, but a little leadership would be appreciated.

Otherwise, I am happy to report that the road to hell is again paved with good intentions. ✳

THE BAGHDAD SHOES FLY IN OUR FACE, TOO

Column, Dec. 17, 2008

There is much rejoicing in certain quarters that an Arab journalist threw his shoes at President George W. Bush in a Baghdad news conference Sunday.

We are all invited to join in the fun — and, yes, it is some kind of ironic fun.

However, I think I will decline the invitation, thank you very much.

It's not just because I think the Worst President in History(TM) isn't worth the waste of comfortable footwear.

It's not because I think the only missiles journalists should launch are sharp-tipped words packaged in bludgeoning phrases.

No, it's mostly because when anyone, especially a foreign national, physically attacks the president of the United States, be it with shoes, sandals, socks, bras, jockstraps, cream pies or anything else absurd or smelly that comes to hand, then it is an assault on the dignity of all of us, even if some of us are not very dignified.

This rule applies to any president and I will brook no opposition on this point. The office demands respect even when the person doesn't.

That George Bush is the King Midas of chaos — everything he touches becomes a golden screw-up — is not in serious dispute. That he has made such a bloody mess of Iraq that shoe-throwers are instantly elevated to the status of heroes is yet another proof of his talent for incompetence.

That is all beside the point. You can say that his own actions earned him the contempt of toe-exposing people everywhere. But, my friends, we are the ones who put him in office.

In short, say not for whom the shoe flies, it flies for thee.

But, thee might say, I did not vote for the man! Well, I didn't either. But collectively enough Americans did vote for him that we are all shamed by this late rain of boots adding a postscript to the footprints of history. There are not enough shoes and sandals in Iraq to make the point of our joint responsibility that this man is in office.

To be sure, the 2000 election was disputed, but it should never have been close. What were people thinking that they wanted someone whose worldview was as fractured as his syntax? They did not put country first.

Then Americans turned around and repeated the folly in 2004. Again, people had their excuses — after all, John Kerry was about as appealing as canvas underpants — but this does not let anyone off the hook (or shoe horn).

In Iraq, we are told, hitting someone with a shoe is among the worst of insults. In our culture, the worst insult to the national intelligence is to fail to kick someone out of office when he or she richly deserves it. This is what we did not do.

We are the ones who put his boots in the White House — and what boots they were, clown boots that slapped the Oval Office floor amid little honks from the vice president's trumpet. This is our fault. We should all have instinctively ducked when the footwear went flying in Baghdad.

The trouble with America is that we have lost all sense of responsibility. We blame everyone else but ourselves when we suffer the slings and arrows of outrageous footwear.

Of course, George Bush betrays no clue that he understands the significance of the incident, but that is entirely within character. While he appears unembarrassed, I, for one, feel the slap of boot leather against my chastened face.

My craft or subtle art failed to make the American people laugh their way to wisdom. I failed! I failed! Please do not throw socks at me. I can stand shoes but a journalist's socks are ghastly unlaundered things and I am at least remorseful.

The other shoe may never drop for this president in his cocoon of incomprehension. But that is not a luxury we share.

In eight years, hardly anyone has been allowed to make any passionate criticism to this president's face. Anyone who wanted to raise an objection was shunted off to a free-speech zone far away from his designated route — in reality, a no-speech zone safely out of the reach of a shout, let alone a well-aimed Top-Sider.

IN iRAQ, *we are told, hitting someone with a shoe is among the worst of insults. In our culture, the worst insult to the national intelligence is to fail to kick someone out of office when he or she richly deserves it. This is what we did not do.*

As I say, I do not approve of throwing anything at any president, not only because it might hit him but also because it might hit us sitting complacent in our shame. ✽

NOT YOUR EVERYDAY INAUGURATION

Column, Jan. 21, 2009

Inaugurations are extraordinary events. They are as much for the people as for the new president, which is as it should be. We the people want to be involved, and not just because we are desperate for entertainment in the dead of winter.

When you stop to think about it, most of us will go through life without ever being inaugurated for anything, let alone president of the United States.

The average person will be birthed, inspected, injected, baptized, circumcised (not available to all customers), inducted, possibly indicted, romanced, rejected, engaged, married, graduated, selected, hired, fired, deluded, outsourced, downsized, medicated, retired and even installed if one is an officer of an Elks or Moose lodge.

But mostly not inaugurated.

(As for me, I have always wanted to be installed. While it sounds like what happens to a kitchen appliance, that at least would be a sign someone considers me useful.)

Not only is inauguration reserved for select company, but it is something that life really doesn't prepare anyone for. So it was especially interesting to watch the novice inaugural candidate, Barack Obama, go through the metaphorical sheep dip yesterday to become our new president.

I thought he handled it with an easy grace. He was serenely self-confident. It was as if inauguration were a regular event in his life and not what it really resembles: A ceremonial root canal performed without anesthetic in a dentist's office where the heat has failed and the whole waiting room is watching to cheer.

But as much as his obvious eloquence, Mr. Obama has the gift of natural dignity. This is what separates him from most of us. I don't know about you, but I could not be installed as Exalted Moose without knocking the microphone over with my nose.

The worst that happened yesterday was a little fumble between the new president and Chief Justice John Roberts over the wording of the presidential oath. Obviously, we shall have to go back to the tape but I think Mr. Obama may have pledged to take the chief justice as his lawful wedded wife, in which case they will have to move the White House to Massachusetts. Michelle may have something to say about it.

At least he didn't use that huge Bible that Joe Biden placed his hand upon during his swearing-in as vice president. I would be afraid to swear anything on that Bible. Clearly, it grew that large because it contains many extra commandments. Frankly, most of us are hard put keeping the 10 regular ones.

In Mr. Biden's case, we can only hope that "Thou shalt not talk the leg off a piano" is one of the extra commandments.

Talking about vice presidents, we saw Dick Cheney make his farewell to the nation while sitting in a wheelchair. He deserves our sympathy. Apparently he was doing his own packing and hurt his back while picking up his pitchforks, racks and thumbscrews. Heck, those items can be heavy.

As for his erstwhile boss, the 43rd president who shall remain nameless because the country has suffered enough, he was gracious at the end so I will make no further potshots. Anyway, he is now officially out of season.

AT LEAST HE DIDN'T USE THAT HUGE BIBLE

that Joe Biden placed his hand upon during his swearing-in as vice president. I would be afraid to swear anything on that Bible. Clearly, it grew that large because it contains many extra commandments. Frankly, most of us are hard put keeping the 10 regular ones.

What a scene the day presented! To viewers all across America and indeed the world, it looked like a sea of waving humanity stretching from the Capitol to at least the Washington Monument.

At the sight of those brave patriots gathered out there in the cold, it was impossible not to think great thoughts about America. This is a land where anybody can grow up to be president — ask Barack Obama. For that matter, this is a land where anybody can grow up to be a millionaire — for this, I am reasonably certain you could ask the guy with the Port-a-Potty concession.

The natural thought that came immediately to mind was this: Thank goodness we are here in a warm room and not out there shivering in our frosted boots while blowing our patriotic noses. The trouble with crowds is that they are too crowded.

I don't know how anyone can make a speech to such a vast assembly. You can't tell a joke because if it bombs, millions of people mutter mirthlessly.

This is why the average person like myself is not suitable for inauguration. It takes confidence, stamina and a better class of thermal underwear to be inaugurated.

Speaking as one of many who was only birthed, inspected, injected, rejected and not even installed, I think we the people picked the right one among us to be inaugurated. This was a happy day in America. ✖

JOE BIDEN PLAYS HIS OWN HAPPY, OFF-KEY TUNE

Column, July 15, 2009

While certainly interesting, the Senate confirmation hearing for Supreme Court nominee Sonia Sotomayor has been lacking one key element for lovers of the genre.

That would be Joe Biden.

When then-Sen. Biden was a longtime member of the Senate Judiciary Committee, you could always count on him to talk the leg off a piano.

Indeed, Washington-area pianists who prized their Steinway would support the piano with trusses when it was the senator's turn to speak. Why, it sometimes happened that pianos in the provinces would fall down in a heap of discordant notes if someone left the televised hearing on.

It is true that the Senate Judiciary Committee has many distinguished gas bags who would never dream of using one short word when 10 long ones were available. Their problem is that they think confirmation hearings are all about them.

But none of these eminent figures has the ability to seriously harm musical instruments or furniture like Sen. Biden did. Oh, I am not saying that a small crack wouldn't appear in a nearby coffee table now and again, due to the sheer weight of pomposity heavy in the air, but this is kid's stuff by Sen. Biden's old standards.

Sic transit gloria mundi an observer might say. As you know, this famous Latin expression means: "Thus passes away the glorious windbags."

Fortunately, all is not lost. Mr. Biden, the scourge of piano owners, is now playing a new if sometimes familiar tune as vice president of the United States, where he serves the commander in chief as the gaffe-maker in chief.

Of course, some will say — mostly idle types suffering from Talk Radio Overdose Syndrome — that President Barack Obama makes his own gaffes. Yes, he does, but again not quite with the happy, spontaneous, to-heck-with-consequences style that Mr. Biden brings to the task. He's no ordinary Joe when it comes to verbal blunders.

He couldn't wait to start. Even on the campaign trail, he not-so-helpfully declared: "Mark my words. Mark my words. It will not be six months before the world tests Barack Obama like they did John Kennedy."

Actually, those who marked these words will further mark that the president hasn't had a Bay of Pigs moment six months into the job. But he has had a few Peninsula of Turkeys clarifications, thanks to his happy-go-lucky sidekick. Two recently came in just one week.

First, Mr. Biden said the administration had misread the economy. (No, Mr. Obama said later, "We had incomplete information.") Then Mr. Biden seemed to give the green light for Israel to attack Iran's nuclear facilities if it wanted to. (Absolutely not, Mr. Obama said later).

This multiple placing of feet in mouth is not to me a sign of the vice president lacking intelligence. On the contrary, he shows signs of being smart — although not to the extent that he knows when to shut up already. Rather, it illustrates the law of averages in action — to wit, the more you talk, the greater the chance that you will say something stupid.

In my memory, nobody ever accused Vice President Dick Cheney of uttering a chance remark that came out wrong. In

Mr. Cheney's case, things came out wrong because they were coldly calculated remarks, or so many of us peasants concluded during that imperial era.

What an interesting contrast these two vice presidents make — Joe Biden, the garrulous clown prince in the public eye, and Dick Cheney, the plotting Rasputin in an undisclosed location.

Of course, once upon a time, vice presidents were minor figures in the scheme of things. The most exciting thing that happened in their lives was when the maid came by to give them an occasional dusting.

> ## WHAT AN INTERESTING CONTRAST
>
> *these two vice presidents make — Joe Biden, the garrulous clown prince in the public eye, and Dick Cheney, the plotting Rasputin in an undisclosed location.*

Mr. Cheney broke that mold as the first vice president to be co-president, even as he served in the shadows often unobserved, all the better to hide his pitchforks and stir his sulphur pot.

In my opinion, and remember I write a lot so I am bound to write something stupid, Joe Biden serves his president better than Dick Cheney served his. It may be heresy to say so, but George W. Bush was a better president when in his last year he appeared to heed his vice president's counsel less.

Yes, better the silly gaffe than the sinister whisper. That is not to say that I think the amusingly talkative Joe Biden would ever make a good successor to Barack Obama. That would be throwing caution and pianos to the wind — and you don't have to be a wise Latina woman to know so. ✤

A HELL OF A WAY TO INTERPRET THE CONSTITUTION

Column, Feb. 23, 2011

Harry S. Truman, the 33rd president of the United States, was a person somewhat unappreciated in his own time — and aren't we all, really. Among many great distinctions, he had some quirky ones.

He kept a sign that said "The buck stops here" on his desk. His middle initial "S." didn't stand for anything (maybe bought with one of the bucks that stopped at his desk).

He appeared in a famously wrong newspaper headline, "Dewey Defeats Truman," on the front page of the Chicago Tribune in 1948. This may be the biggest mistake made in a newspaper, quite a feat in an industry that has raised the correction/clarification to a high art with, not to boast, no small help from me.

I call Harry S. Truman today as my first and only witness in the case of selective national amnesia, the real source of all our problems. Americans have forgotten much of their own history. For many, whole sections of the past have passed into oblivion.

As the great man is not here to testify in person — even allowing for inflation, a buck does not buy immortality — a speech he made on Dec. 15, 1952, will have to suffice. President Truman was speaking at the National Archives to dedicate a new shrine holding the Constitution, the Declaration of Independence and the Bill of Rights. Consider this passage from his remarks, which suggest that people were a whole lot smarter 60 years ago:

"The Constitution expresses an idea that belongs to the people — the idea of the free man. What this idea means may vary from time to time. There was a time when people believed that the Constitution meant that men could not be prevented from exploiting child labor or paying sweatshop wages," Truman said.

"We no longer believe these things. We have discovered that the Constitution does not prevent us from correcting social injustice, or advancing the general welfare. The idea of freedom which is embodied in these great documents has overcome all attempts to turn them into a rigid set of rules to suppress freedom."

Not so fast, Mr. President. If you had lived in our brain-dead time, you would find that a host of people most definitely do believe that the Constitution can't be used to correct social injustice or advance the general welfare, as the opposition to universal health care makes clear.

These critics mostly remember the 18th century.

They make a fetish of studying it, but only to reinforce their idea that the Constitution is an ancient corset, with a rigid set of rules as its whalebone stays, and all for the purpose of keeping voluptuous outbreaks of justice and the general welfare from shocking the landed gentry.

As for the 19th and early 20th centuries, when monopolist-minded tycoons made many ordinary people feel that freedom was a choice between working for a pittance or starving, these Constitution zealots know nothing of that.

In Pittsburgh, we tend to remember these unpleasant truths because a lot of labor's battles were fought in this region. Also, some of our Democratic politicians are a bit dated. If you ask them what time it is, they say, "Half past the 19th century" — which is ridiculous because every Republican diehard knows the correct time is half past the 18th century.

With everybody either forgetting history entirely or else editing it in their heads, committing to memory the useful bits and forgetting the rest, it is amazing what the nation has forgotten.

For example, the buck doesn't stop at the president's desk anymore. It no more stopped at George W. Bush's desk for wrecking the economy than it does at Barack Obama's desk for stimulating it without great success.

THEY MAKE A FETISH OF STUDYING IT,

but only to reinforce their idea that the Constitution is an ancient corset, with a rigid set of rules as its whalebone stays, and all for the purpose of keeping voluptuous outbreaks of justice and the general welfare from shocking the landed gentry.

In Wisconsin, Gov. Scott Walker's idea of history is apparently the presidency of Ronald Reagan and the idea that if you get tough with the union movement and also cut taxes, then deficits will disappear — except in Reagan's case, they didn't.

In the governor's history, unions are not heirs to those who built the American middle class but dangerous budget-busting freeloaders such as public school teachers. And what could be more dangerous than someone forcing biology lessons upon children? (Maybe Wall Street bankers who give themselves bonuses after taking the public's money? Just a thought.)

In Congress, the people's mandate for fiscally responsible change has been extended to include wholesale attacks on the Environmental Protection Agency for daring to insist on clean air. Thus it seems that even the historic idea of America the Beautiful has become victim to selective ideological amnesia — *"O beautiful for spacious skies filled with pollution."*

If only Harry were still around to give 'em hell. ✹

VOTE FOR ME, GOP:
A PRESIDENTIAL PLATFORM

Column, May 18, 2011

I take the opportunity today to declare my intention to seek the Republican nomination for president.

Many candidates make a grand event of this, but that is not my humble nature. Nor do I wish to employ so-called "new media," such as Twitter and Facebook. Those newfangled gimmicks are for the likes of Barack Obama. You will want me to use a Teleprompter next.

Such a momentous announcement as mine should not be tweeted like a canary commenting on a bird feeder. As for Facebook, I have no desire to make a book of my face. People suffer enough when they meet me.

No, I am appealing to old-fashioned folks nostalgic for the days when carrier pigeons did a fine job of carrying messages. I want real conservatives, backward-thinking folks steeped in the ways of the past — not to mention steeped in alcoholic beverages taken strictly for medicinal purposes.

This is my target demographic. Nothing against young people, but my view is that they are not yet smart enough to be old. Instead of sitting around texting each other on whatever comes into their young heads, they should be preparing themselves for all the national debt they are destined to inherit. Many seniors agree with me about this.

Why, you ask, have I decided to run at this time? Because I hear my nation calling me to service. "Yoo-hoo, Reg," the nation says. I must say it startled me when I first heard it. I thought it was my wife telling me to mow the lawn.

The other reason I am running is that the Republican field is being reduced by the minute. This is very worrisome. If this keeps up, political pundits will have nothing to comment about. They will become like Trappist monks in their contemplative silence, only less pious.

Donald Trump has withdrawn, as if taking a whole weather system off the map, his hair alone having served as a vast cloud front. Mike Huckebee has also departed — and gone with him is the down-home jovial presence much admired by those who prefer gravy to gravitas.

The field hasn't become too bland, not with the serially repentant Newt Gingrich making the case that everything the party of family values has stood for in the last 20 years will be revealed as hypocritical if he is nominated.

And he is just one of a madcap crew, such as Michele Bachmann, who is so clever that she can make up history, and Rick Santorum, famous for his principled stand against inter-species sex.

This is all very well, but if President Obama is to be defeated, the Republican Party cannot turn its back on the stodgy views and sclerotic prejudices that have made the GOP great. So what does that whippersnapper Rep. Paul Ryan think he is up to with his vouchers for Medicare? Where is the old-fashioned pandering?

Someone special needs to run for president to stop the rot. Did I say I love America? And adore dogs and old people, not necessarily in that order? (I am still working out my position on kittens.)

As a bonus, no doubt exists on whether I was born in this country — and for good reason. I wasn't. By geographical chance, I was born in Singapore and grew up in Australia, but I believe I am a natural-born citizen because I have been called "a natural" many times — most recently, a "natural screw-up."

SOMEONE SPECIAL *needs to run for president to stop the rot. Did I say I love America? And adore dogs and old people, not necessarily in that order? (I am still working out my position on kittens.*

Besides, who knows what "natural born" means in the Constitution? You can't be president if your mother had a Caesarean? This is clearly a job for lawyers. When I hire some at $300 an hour, the American people will recognize this as one of the most fundamentally patriotic acts in the United States of Attorneys. That should quell the controversy.

As befitting my modern-averse candidacy, I am working out position papers that will comfort voters with a strong resistance to change. I have decided to support the gold standard but oppose the Treaty of Versailles.

On more contemporary issues, I believe wrinkles should be tax deductible and Medicare and Social Security should be declared religions that cannot be taxed or interfered with. It is true that I am for bringing back the stocks, but only for the crime of cell phone use in theaters. However, I am against debtor prisons because everybody in America would have to be put in one.

I thank you for your support. Look for my exciting slogan ("Back to the Future") and political announcements delivered by friendly carrier pigeons. Talk about tweeting. ✸

GAY MARRIAGE LOOKS LIKE LATEST PHONY THREAT

Column, June 14, 2014

Last month, my wife and I celebrated our 38th wedding anniversary, but it's not clear to me what (if any) name this anniversary has.

Certainly, it's not golden or silver. Maybe it's something suitably romantic for our domestic situation, such as the linoleum anniversary or the kitchen appliances anniversary.

All I can say is that we are continuing to be happily married, despite the many challenges of married life. For example, she has observed that I am a poor driver and speak with my mouth full at the dinner table. This is nonsense, of course, and I would refute these charges if only my mouth weren't full.

But late last month, a new challenge to our marriage arose. A federal judge ruled that gay couples would be allowed to marry in Pennsylvania. Previously, marriage was defined by law in the traditional way as being between one man with his mouth full and one woman who points it out.

But U.S. District Judge John E. Jones III, an appointee of President George W. Bush, found the law banning same-sex marriage to be unconstitutional. To those of you who are new to the commonwealth or live somewhere where the 19th century and its social customs have already lifted, you cannot imagine how extraordinary this news was.

You could have knocked people over with a feather. In fact, people made a point of not walking near poultry farms in case a stray feather felled them in their tracks. Gay marriage in socially conservative Pennsylvania? Get-outta-here!

But it happened — and I say thank goodness for the triumph of logic, which is something that doesn't happen nearly enough. It was plainly ridiculous that heterosexuals could get married and divorced multiple times, in ceremonies perhaps featuring Elvis impersonators, and the sanctity of marriage would be preserved, yet that wouldn't be the case if a gay couple attempted the same thing.

Immediately after the judge's ruling, however, long-married people like myself were put on alert. After all, we had been warned.

As advanced by various moralizers and self-righteous busybodies, one argument against gay marriage was that the very existence of marriage would be subverted if same-sex couples became eligible to wed. It was certainly frightening to think that my own marriage would be imperiled after my wife's years of effort to bring me to a state of perfection, a work obviously still in progress.

But now a couple of weeks have passed and things are remarkably calm and undisturbed. On my dutiful stroll to take the trash out, in the time-honored way of husbands, I find that the bins are not full of torn moral fiber or ripped social fabric.

On the street, there are no obvious signs of moral decay, just common domesticity as usual. And further afield, instead of general sadness there's joy among those long excluded from one of the fundamental rights of ordinary Americans and deprived no more.

The news from Pennsylvania is that there is no news. Most people don't much care. The extraordinary has become ordinary. My marriage is no more threatened by gays being wed than it is by the threat of aliens coming down in space ships and tempting my wife by driving better, in this or any galaxy, and not speaking with their tentacles full.

I suppose we shouldn't have been surprised. Those opposed to progressive social change have always invented horror stories that inevitably don't come true. Get the kids out of the mines and they will become hopelessly spoiled. Let the women vote and they will have no judgment. Pass Social Security and the elderly will become idle in their golden years. Pass universal health care and the nation will be lost.

So much for all of that. So many horror stories, so little actual horror. If only some of these conservative guardians would speak with mouths full at the dinner table, they wouldn't be able to fit a foot in their mouths. As it is, future generations will marvel that conservatism was here defined as denying some Americans basic rights. ✳

IT WAS PLAINLY RIDICULOUS

that heterosexuals could get married and divorced multiple times, in ceremonies perhaps featuring Elvis impersonators, and the sanctity of marriage would be preserved, yet that wouldn't be the case if a gay couple attempted the same thing.

It's not that gay marriage has been universally accepted throughout the United States; not even a majority of states have it and the U.S. Supreme Court has only partially approved it. But if stodgy old Pennsylvania can do it, any state can, and that's enough for me to celebrate. They called a culture war and the culture of greater freedom won.

Congratulations to all the newlyweds who have benefited. I hope you stay happily married until your kitchen appliance anniversary. ✺

ABOUT THE AUTHOR

Reg Henry is an award-winning columnist for the Pittsburgh Post-Gazette. His work has appeared in more than 150 newspapers in the United States, causing laughter and dismay depending on whether readers have understood the jokes. As his sense of humor is dry, an adult beverage can assist in comprehension.

Born in Singapore, he grew up in Australia where he first entered journalism, served in the Australian Army in Vietnam, went to England and worked on The Times of London and then met his American wife-to-be who brought him to the United States. He was as surprised as she was at this turn of events.

He joined the Post-Gazette in 1978 but later spent five years in California as editor of The Monterey County Herald before returning to Pittsburgh. He is the PG's deputy editorial page editor and the column is a holiday from his regular work. He plans one day soon to move back to California and live happily ever after in the sun.

WA